DALLAS COP

VOLUME III

300 TRUE SHORT STORIES

RAY DETHLOFF

Book cover design by The Book Cover Whisperer:
OpenBookDesign.biz

979-8-2183-7882-0 ISBN

This book is dedicated to the shocking number of Police Officers that have died in the line of duty in the history of the United States. Since the first recorded in 1791, the startling total has been 26,547.*

* ODMP – Officer Down Memorial Page as of 03/01/2024

Readers,

DALLAS COP Volume III is the final book to complete my trilogy of DALLAS COP books. As in Volume II, *DALLAS COP Volume III* has no chapters. From the first true story until the last, there are 300 in total here, bringing the aggregate of all three *DALLAS COP* book stories to be over 800.

 The completion of this book is also the fulfillment of a decades-long goal to publish my many true crime/police stories. I appreciate your loyalty and patronage. Enjoy. Thank you!

Sincerely, Ray Dethloff

Dallas Cop (Retired)

DALLAS COP VOLUME III

Christmas Day, 1995. Half of the officers on my shift came in at 8 a.m., the other half wouldn't be in until 12 noon. A half day for all with full pay. It should be slow enough for that to be feasible, not a day that we would expect to be inundated with calls for service.

An hour into our shift, an officer spotted an occupied stolen vehicle, and I rushed to assist him. Just after I arrived, together we took his suspect into custody. Soon after I rushed to assist some other officers who were having problems with a drunk male firing numerous bullets from his pistol while outside on his second-floor balcony. He was throwing bottles into the air as targets and trying to shoot them down. He had missed and struck some other buildings with his dangerous gunplay. All total, the gunman had popped off about 20 rounds. As I drove up to the other side of this shooter's building, a sergeant did too, but this sergeant had just arrived after driving to the location code 3. He meant to turn off his siren, but accidentally alerted the shooter to our nearby presence when he inadvertently turned on the P.A. system when he moved the selector switch one notch too far, allowing the police radio to blast through his speaker. A concealed officer reported that the suspect then slipped back inside his apartment. I went with three other officers and tried shouting Spanish from the first floor to persuade someone to open the second-floor front door, but I was probably not heard over the heavy bass music from their apartment. A Spanish-speaking officer arrived from a different patrol division and tried speaking with him. We all moved to the top of the stairs and the perpetrator door opened. I burst inside, weapon at the ready, with all other officers behind me and shouted "Manos Arriba!" (Hands up!). I bypassed the man who opened the door knowing the other officers were behind me and entered another room (we had earlier learned that 10 men lived in this apartment). There were four sleeping or pretending to sleep. In Spanish, I yelled "Policia!" and ordered them to put up their hands, then we quickly pulled away the covers and looked under the pillows and mattresses but could not find a pistol. We assembled the eight males that we found in the living room. Another officer found the pistol lying in the fireplace. Only a couple of them spoke limited English, and when asked which of the men did the shooting from the balcony, they both lied and told us that that man had left the apartment that we had surrounded. The Spanish speaking officer spoke to them as well, but I could tell by his calm non-threatening tone that the males were not intimidated at all to tell us the truth and give us the shooter identity. The shirt that the suspect had been wearing on the balcony had been removed, and there were now four shirtless males among the eight men. No one wanted to claim the pistol and even had the audacity to say that they didn't know how a pistol got into their fireplace. A few dozen empty beer cans were atop the kitchen table and on the floor nearby. We couldn't arrest anyone for UCW (Unlawfully Carrying a Weapon), discharging a weapon inside the city limits, or Public Intoxication, so all we did was place the pistol in our property room as Found Property.

A 72-year-old man drove into a dog park parking lot, then got out and urinated in public. After lingering around his car for a time, an anonymous person called the police thinking that he might be drunk. The old man said he was a diabetic, so an ambulance was called because it was 3:30 p.m. and maybe he just had low blood sugar making him seem drunk. No, he was drunk. From central Europe, he still had a heavy accent even after having lived here 30 years. We took him to Detox. He kept asking us what was happening and what we were doing, he wasn't drunk, he would be calling his lawyer, and that the ladies loved him. "See? The ladies love me and can't keep their hands off me because I have a big dick", then showed us. The crass, crude and lewd drunk would be kept there a minimum of 6 hours.

A man never really recovered from the loss of both of his parents in a short time. His wife arrived home from work to discover a suicide note indicating that he was going to the lake to kill himself. This surprised her because she had just spoken to him by phone after lunch and he had seemed fine. Now she was worried that he had his pistol, and she called the police. I was one of the officers at the lake that evening, and we began looking for his car around 7 p.m. My friend found his empty car, and we began trekking through the high grass and the woods near the parking lot to find him. Just as it was starting to get too dark for visibility without a flashlight, the other officer retraced some steps in an area and almost stepped on his corpse. He had shot himself, but we couldn't find the pistol anywhere near his lifeless body. I asked our helicopter to use their FLIR equipment to see if they had any thermal imaging from his body heat signature. There was none, so he'd been dead for several hours in the mid-50's temperature. When the Medical Examiner rolled him over from being face down, there was his pistol; he'd fallen on it.

Ironically, his car had a "Life is Good" window decal.

While working at Sam's Club, I was told by an employee that a man was spitting on the floor. What kind of an uncultured jerk does that? I walked over to where he was standing in line and watched him spit again on the concrete floor. A third world immigrant, he looked like he had a bad attitude and he seemed so indifferent about his spitting. I told him that it was nasty and disgusting, that he needed to clean it up, and I gave him a paper towel from under a cashier's register. He reluctantly gave the floor a quick wipe. We gazed at each other with disdain and scorn until his friend finished checking out and they left. A couple of shocked customers told me that they had never seen anyone spit indoors before, and I hadn't either.

I covered an officer at a traffic stop. He had a motorist who proudly stated that he was a "sovereign citizen" in Texas, and he didn't have to obey any authority except the County Sheriff. Texas was still a sovereign nation, and he would obey no city or federal police. He was forcibly arrested after locking his arms out in a passively resistant attempt to impede us. As a group, his kind was very litigious. We were sued, and in the lawsuit, I was specifically called a "Devil's Minion". The case was dismissed, as eventually they all were because of needlessly clogging up the court system with so many frivolous lawsuits.

Some of them had been involved in counterfeiting. I knew this, so I had put a "Hold" on many silver dollar coins he had in his possession until an expert could examine them for their authenticity. It took him seven years to get his real coins back.

An alarm at a business indicated an open door. I arrived and found the front door to be unlocked, but the posted business hours indicated that they were closed. I entered. I quickly U-turned and made an adrenaline-fueled dash to the door, a big snarling dog at my heels. Bolting out that door, I turned to face him as I reached for my pistol and realized that he had stopped suddenly at the door because he was at the end of his chain, snarling and barking. Relieved, that was the closest that I ever came to shooting a dog.

A friend and his rookie arrived quickly at a 41-11 (Burglary in progress), and at gunpoint took two of the three burglars into custody as they struggled to descend from the balcony of the second-floor apartment which they had just burglarized. A third suspect escaped and ran when they approached, but they had broadcasted his description even before stopping. I covered them on the call and there were few people outside in the complex on this hot day. Spotting a male sitting a few steps up a stairwell, I stopped to ascertain if he was my suspect. He was sweating profusely and holding onto a removed t-shirt the same color as worn by the burglar who fled. I exited my car with a pepper ball gun and stood near the stairwell entrance. Never having had a chance to spray pepper balls at the ground around a fleeing suspect, I was hoping to have my chance today. The pepper balls would explode on impact with the ground, releasing clouds of oleo capsicum pepper powder and engulf any suspect in a choking haze of disabling dust. I radioed my buddy to come over to my building number when they were ready to verify my capture (it was him).

The kid later said he knew what the device was; he had heard stories about it, and decided against running. I had noticed him vacillating in his mind for a couple of minutes as he looked at me, then at the pepper ball gun, again and again. I was ready to let loose, and he knew it. I never had that chance again because the pepper ball guns were decommissioned a short time later.

I spotlighted a vehicle on a November night and saw two figures squirming back and forth in their seats like they were pulling up their pants. I marched to their vehicle, and they were sitting quietly as if nothing had happened. I told them that I could see that something was happening but wasn't sure exactly what and asked what they were doing. The woman replied by saying "We were just hanging ". Only I couldn't discern that last word, and asked "You were doing what?" She replied "Hanging". I smiled and said "Oh. I thought you used a word that started with the letter "B". The man said "Banging?" then smiled and added "C'mon now!"

I arrested a shoplifter at the Sam's Club where I was working as a side job. He started crying in the office, then began hyperventilating, telling me that he had a hard time breathing and had a pain in his chest. I believed him to be feigning an emergency, but if I was wrong and there was a death in my custody because of my refusing to order an ambulance it would all be on me. I ordered the ambulance and told him that because the theft was a misdemeanor, he needed to call police when he was released so they could take him to the county jail. Surprise, he never called.

The Detective assigned to the case asked me how the thief was identified. He had no identification at the time of his arrest, so I had simply used the name and info that the thief had provided me with during his brief office stay. Understandably and rightly so, the Detective would not file the theft case because of uncertainty regarding the true identity of the suspect.

Two months later, I was on duty about 6 miles away from that Sam's Club sitting in my parked police car typing a report. I was distracted by a man who got out of his car carrying a bag of groceries to an apartment door. It was him! I exited my car and called over to him. He stopped, and I reminded him of how we knew each other. He apologized, saying that he had just moved to Texas at that time and was staying with his sister, and didn't want to be in any trouble. I had him give me ID--which he now had--and informed him that we were going back to the police station to speak with the Detective and straighten this out. Once there, he provided a written statement to the same Detective, honorably confessing to that theft two months earlier, and I took him to jail.

A few of us drove code 3 out to Lake Ray Hubbard. Another officer had walked up to a seated male facing the lake in his car and withdrew after seeing a pistol on the man's lap. The suspect was parked about 100 yards away from a restaurant on the lake, deep in the parking lot where few cars were parked. Attempts to communicate with him were unproductive. While we were waiting for SWAT to arrive, some of us heard an unremarkable "Pop". The man had shot himself in the head to commit suicide.

It was the evening of New Year's Eve.

Several friends were partying together and consumed a lot of alcohol. A girl from that group went next door to a neighbor's apartment and started talking to the guy that lived there. They finished talking after a while and the tenant went to sleep in his room, while the drunken girl fell asleep on his couch after having passed out from drinking too much. Later, the tenant's brother returned home from work and found an attractive girl sleeping on the couch. He tried to awaken her to find out who she was and what she was doing in their apartment. No use, she was passed out drunk. He decided not to let this opportunity pass, so he had sex with her while she was unconscious. The next day, he told his brother he had raped her (though not using that word). The brother promptly went next door to where the girl lived and told her and her roommates what his brother had done to her. She had no idea until that moment.

We arrived and told the suspect that a sexual assault case was going to be filed against him, and not to leave town. He could not be arrested at that time because too many hours had ticked away since the actual crime, which was hearsay.

Friends of the victim took her to Parkland Hospital where she underwent a rape examination.

The manager of a check cashing business kept the Dallas Morning News Crimestoppers picture of a man that was wanted for forgery in the off chance that he happened to walk into the business to try to cash a stolen check. Walk in he did, and the manager came out from around the counter and held the suspect at gunpoint until I arrived. The manager made some

Crime Stoppers reward money that day, while the suspect went to jail for his forgery warrant, a probation violation, a bit of marijuana, and some ticket warrants.

I was driving out of the park when I read the comments of a 911 call in a nearby neighborhood indicating that an older man wearing a red knit hat and black clothes looked to be confused and was wandering aimlessly. I had just seen a 60-ish male matching that description walking down the bike trail seconds earlier. I circled back and exited my car to speak to him. He didn't have any ID and said that he was trying to get to his sister's house. The problem was that he didn't know what direction he was going and didn't have her address memorized. He really was lost. I asked him for his name, and he replied "Sammy Davis Jr." "Sure you are. Look, just give me your real name so that I can help you." "Officer, that is my real name". Still thinking that I was dealing with someone who was a delusional member of the "Rat Pack", just for kicks I suspect-checked that name and the provided birthday on my laptop. Stunned, I saw that his sister had reported him as a missing person. At White Rock Lake where he was found he was over 20 miles away and had been gone for 4 days. I phoned her and told her that I had found him and that he was just fine. She screamed out loud and I heard her telling someone that "They found him! They found him!" It took a minute for her to calm down and stop crying her tears of joy. I arranged for her to come and retrieve him several miles away at a 7-Eleven rendezvous point. She showed up smiling and crying and gave me a hug and thanked me after she hugged him. He was smiling for the first time since he'd been with me and was happy to be going home. They'd had a petty argument, and he left the house to go for a long walk, but then couldn't find his way home. I called the Reporting Person/911 caller to tell him what had happened and that just as he speculated, the man had been lost and in need of help.

While working at Sam's Club, the Walmart officer upstairs called and asked me if I could help detain thieves that Loss Prevention was monitoring on their surveillance cameras. We brought them back to the office when they tried to leave with hundreds of dollars' worth of stolen property that they had unabashedly stuffed into plastic bags, a suitcase, and their clothes. Our General Orders prohibited male officers from searching females. I lifted the dress of one suspect and found three items stuffed inside the panties, and I pulled down the suspect's blouse and looked inside the bra for any stolen property. I did all of this without violating General Orders. The suspect was a man wearing women's clothing.

I rode my bike under a park pavilion with about 30 people present, about a dozen of them drinking beer from cans and bottles. After getting their attention by announcing "Excuse Me" twice, I informed them that drinking alcohol in city parks was illegal, and that those with alcohol needed to pour it out. Two men from the group walked to a trash can, but then drank what was left in their bottles AFTER I had just told them it was illegal to consume alcohol in a Dallas Park. I wrote them both a ticket. One wanted to argue that he did pour it out, but I reminded him that he poured it in, as in into his mouth. A woman walked over to me and said that this was her 4-year-old son's birthday party (there were very few children, mostly adults). The party was just an excuse for the adults to drink alcohol on a weekend. It was obvious it wasn't for the kids. She chided me, saying for future reference that I could be more discreet. When I asked for her advice on how I could do that, she was speechless and walked away.

A complainant observed his stolen vehicle being driven by an unknown male. He and his friend followed the suspect to a house and called the police. Just before we arrived, a woman had backed out of the driveway, but they couldn't follow her because they wanted to show police the house. We arrived, and just several minutes later, the female driver returned and stepped out of the car with a bag of groceries. We drove up to the woman and yelled at her to not enter the house. Visually frightened, she complied. We told her that she was in a stolen vehicle, and she replied that it wasn't hers, that it belonged to a guy inside her house and that we could go inside and get him. We roused him from his slumber and arrested him for driving the stolen vehicle. The woman explained that she had let this man and his girlfriend stay at her house two weeks ago, and they arrived in that car. It had keys so she never thought it might be stolen.

The arrestee had no ID and was warned that he would be fingerprinted so if he was lying about his name, we would find out and add another charge. Like so many knuckleheads, he didn't listen, and we ended up filing an additional charge of Failing to ID as a Fugitive since he had some warrants.

The arrestee had no money at the time of his book-in. He was brought to the male hold over tank which at that time had no chairs, being just a concrete floor where arrested men sat and stood awaiting arraignment by a judge. Before we had even left the jail, we were told that another prisoner had reported that he was missing $36. That exact sum of money was found in our penniless prisoner's pocket. Jail personnel generated a theft report to be added to our charges against him.

I wrote a speeding ticket to a woman who said that it was worth it because she was hurrying home to watch the Dallas Cowboys game.

I arrived at an accident scene on LBJ Freeway and could see that a Fire Engine was blocking the right lane up ahead to shield those involved in the accident, and the first officer that arrived had stopped about 200 yards behind it. They were at a curve, and it was difficult for motorists to see the accident and then move from the right lane to another lane. I positioned myself back further, hoping that approaching motorists could see me in the right lane and give them a heads up on the lane closure up ahead. I soon realized that was also at a curve and in a dangerous spot. Motorists couldn't always merge smoothly by going to a non-right lane, so I wisely moved my police car with emergency lights to the right side of the shoulder; at least the right lane where I had been was open now and hopefully people would notice the need to move left. The Fire Engine and Ambulance left, leaving the lead police car still partly blocking the right lane up ahead. More and more cars were now having trouble merging to the left, and some now started to stop in the right lane. Drivers were now coming around the bend confronted by my flashing emergency lights on the road shoulder to then see backed up bumper-to-bumper traffic in the right lane of about 10 vehicles. Some had to brake hard. A huge cement mixer truck came around the bend and knew with his heavy load that he didn't have enough stopping distance. He swerved right to avoid the last car in the back up and drove onto the shoulder between the line of cars and my parked car on the right side of the shoulder. He was slowing down, but still barreling towards the other squad car and the cars involved in the accident. They all saw this monstrosity of a truck coming toward them when he was about 50 yards away. I could see them scattering as he got closer. One officer ran to his police car and rapidly accelerated forward as much as he could. The cement truck driver came to a halt on the grassy embankment just right of his police car. The angry officer yelled at the driver, accusing him of not paying attention. I came to the truck driver's aid and declared that he didn't have much reaction time and to the contrary, he did a great job handling his heavy truck.

That night I awoke at 4 a.m. and couldn't get back to sleep. I thought about how multiple people could have died in an inferno, me included. One of the stopped vehicles in that backed up right lane when that large cement truck came around the corner was a flatbed truck filled with propane tanks.

A woman went out to lunch. When she returned, she discovered that someone had pried open her rear door and went to her kitchen. The unknown suspect took out a jar of Vlasic Pickles from the refrigerator and ate all of them, leaving the bottle on the counter. Nothing else was disturbed or stolen. I called for the Physical Evidence Section to hopefully get some latent prints from the jar.

A family had moved to Dallas from New Orleans after Hurricane Katrina. The day before Easter Sunday, Granny was so annoying and adamant about wanting to go back to New Orleans for Easter and to live there that the family loaded her up in their car along with her suitcases at 1 a.m. Easter morning, which was late Saturday Night. This was a high crime complex with many thugs around. It didn't take a genius to realize that they were going on a trip. Shortly after they left, someone broke the patio door glass and gained entry into their apartment, stayed a while, and had many beers. When the family returned home days later, everything was stolen. A bedroom set, three TV's, two love seats, two lamps, two chairs, two tables, and the microwave. Of course, none of the neighbors had seen anything.

A homeless woman had died under a bridge of a drug overdose. A week later, I saw a young man with a white cross under the bridge but on the wrong side. He was the son of the deceased and wanted to pay his respects to his mother by visiting the place where she had died. I directed him to the spot on the other side where she had passed away. It was up the concrete embankment at the very top under the road above. There were still a few items of no value there from his mother, and he placed the small cross atop level concrete at the very top of the underpass where I told him no one would notice. Then he wept.

I stopped a woman for having an expired inspection sticker, and she was arrested for outstanding traffic ticket warrants. We thought it was unusual that she wanted to leave her purse in the car, which was going to be towed. I found a baggie of weed on the floorboard behind her driver seat. Though she was alone, she said it wasn't hers. Neither was the pair of hemostats with the blackened tips from smoking marijuana that was found in her purse.

I switched to working on Thursdays at Sam's Club. A woman was being pointed in my direction. She scurried over to me and in an exasperated, panicked voice told me in accented English "Sir! I go outside and put my food in my truck. My kids were with me. Next, I look, and they are gone! I don't know where they went! What happened to them I don't know! They disappear!!" I thought great, my first Thursday shift and I have a woman whose two kids are gone. Another person who wanted to help also understood her to have said "Kids", but to our relief we soon realized that she had said "Keys" when she told us that she had last put them in the cart. She insinuated that the cart boy who had helped her load her groceries might have taken them, and to pacify her I had him pull out his pant pockets. Minutes later her keys were found in the dark near her car on the hard-to-see blacktop surface. She never apologized to the cart boy.

Sometimes a minor violation of the law like a city ordinance violation can lead to a good arrest, but the key is that an officer must exercise initiative. I was with another bike officer on the bike trail when we spotted two males crossing up ahead carrying beer which is illegal in city parks. One just received a ticket, but the other went to jail for his parole violation warrant.

A suspect was found wandering the streets aimlessly, seemingly dazed and confused. He had possible internal injuries from having struck and killed a Dallas Police Officer on North Central Expressway several hours earlier while driving a stolen car. After being in custody for some time, it was decided that though he had no visible injuries, he would be taken to the hospital to be examined. Two officers from the deceased officer's patrol division would transport and guard this prisoner. Another officer and I were chosen. At the hospital, we were skeptical of his claimed internal injuries, thinking it merely to delay transport to the county jail. We agreed that he must be telling the truth when he was told that a catheter was going to be inserted and he didn't wince.

Later that day, while the prisoner was still undergoing treatment at the hospital, we saw that his sister had come to visit and check on him. Ironically, she was a uniformed Dallas Police Officer.

A married couple had brought their 3 and 6-year-old children with them to the store to go on a theft spree. The mother would point out things on the shelf, and the father would remove the item from the packaging and place it in the diaper bag that she was carrying. They were taken into custody by Loss Prevention. We arrived and found that the man had numerous credit cards that he could have used to buy the merchandise. The woman cried and said they were just doing it to have some fun; they weren't supposed to get caught. They went to jail while their kids went to Child Welfare.

I was inside a young woman's apartment writing down property that had been stolen from her in a burglary. I noticed a couple of tall stacks of Blockbuster Videotapes stacked against her living room wall. Occasionally, I would work as police officer security at some Blockbuster locations, and stacks of 35 videos raised a red flag for me. I inquired as to who owned the tapes, and she replied that her friend did. Her friend used to work for Blockbuster, but moved back home with her mother and didn't want to take them with her. My burglary complainant agreed to hold them for her. This was obviously suspicious to me. I looked at the Blockbuster Store addresses on the video boxes, and they came from 10 different stores. She found me some empty bags so that I could remove all of them from her apartment, and I brought them to the NE Patrol Division, listing her friend as a suspect in a Found Property report that outlined the circumstances. I contacted a Regional Loss Prevention manager who sent a District Manager to the substation to collect the videotapes. When I returned from vacation, I had an appreciative note from Blockbuster and several free rental coupons to reward me for the recovery of the $700 wholesale cost of the videos. In addition, every police station in Dallas was given a supply of free video rental coupons. I'll never know if this was a coincidence, or if my confiscation initiated this Blockbuster thank you gesture to Dallas Police Officers.

A Muslim man purchased several dozen boxes of vegetable oil from Sam's Club with no other items. He paid for the purchase with untraceable gift cards. I had a heightened awareness of suspicious activities since 9/11/2001 and didn't want to simply dismiss this as a large purchase for a restaurant, for example. I knew that vegetable oil was an ingredient used in homemade explosives, so I decided better to err on the side of caution. I obtained this shopper's ID before he left the parking lot and alerted a member of our Criminal Intelligence Unit working in conjunction with the FBI Terrorism Task Force. His investigation determined that this man had bought three vehicles to be sent to Nigeria in a cargo container. He had intended to load a 300-gallon drum of vegetable oil with his vehicles because there were no extra shipping charges, but he was unable to have it in Dallas on time for the shipment, so he bought a large quantity of multi-gallon containers from Sam's. He used gift cards that he had earned from his employer, and except for the vegetable oil alteration, had made this shipment several times before.

In his email, the investigator agreed that the purchase was definitely unusual and appreciated me taking the time to alert them of this suspicious incident so that they could do their job.

A student was causing a disturbance at an elementary school. The Assistant Principal met me in the front parking lot when I arrived. She told me that the boy was upset, grabbed his book bag, and ran outside into the neighborhood. We needed to locate him quickly or he would be a "Critical Missing" because of his age, and police would have to continue looking for him until he was found. I alerted the other officer, and we patrolled the area, even going to his nearby apartment in case he ran home. He didn't. I phoned the school for any updates, and I was told that the boy was back inside the school, but they wanted us to come anyway. We returned to find a little boy looking at us from inside the front door glass. He ran down the hallway to flee from the police (a sign of things to come?). I entered the school to find that the other officer was already in the office with the boy, who was still having a tantrum and bouncing up and down in his chair, red-faced, and pounding his firsts on the arm rests. The story unfolded that the boy had been in his classroom and started breaking pencils. The teacher told him to stop and sit down; he did neither. When the teacher grabbed his arm to guide him back to his chair, be pulled away and then began to kick and punch her. His teacher summoned three other teachers to be witnesses and assisted her in calming down this out-of-control teeny-bopper. The boy punched and kicked them too. The boy's father was called yet again to be told that his son was causing disruption in the school, this time assaulting four teachers. The Assistant Principal told the father that she didn't want him to return to school until the next Thursday. That was a week school suspension for a six-year-old!

I did a Social Services Referral for the little hellion. A week later a social worker called me and said if he caused more problems, then we should put him in the Parkland Hospital Mental Ward where he could vent some steam by bouncing around a rubber padded room. Easy for her to say. I'd be the one possibly vilified by the media for putting a 6 yr. old into a Psych Ward.

A non-English speaking girl in her late teens was having financial problems, so she decided to steal. She rifled through some mail at an apartment complex and managed to get lucky and opened an envelope containing someone else's dividend check. She wanted to cash the check but didn't speak English and didn't drive. She saw a Spanish speaking couple that she had seen earlier and asked them for help with cashing her check. They noticed that the check was from Albertsons, and a store was nearby, so they decided to be good neighbors and drive her there. Once there, the girl went to the counter, and the couple translated for her, indicating her desire to cash the check, but she didn't have any ID. The cashier looked at the check, then notified her supervisor who called the police. I arrested the girl for Forgery. Bizarre coincidence? Fate? Bad luck? The teen girl suspect had actually handed the stolen dividend check to the true owner; the cashier herself had been waiting for that same check to arrive in her mailbox.

I stopped a man for his broken left rear vent window. He had bought it like that and showed me his purchase paperwork. I typed a routine check of his DL on my computer before I cut him loose and found that he had a parole violation and he was going back to prison. I waited for my cover officer to arrive, and then we arrested him after his warrant was confirmed. He had no reaction when I handcuffed him and when I told him why. Minutes later in the patrol car, he decided to protest by telling me that he was not on parole and that I had the wrong guy. This despite his having a picture DL, Social Security Card, and his info with his physical description matching the info on my computer screen. Nice try bubba.

A man had just left the skyscraper where he worked and walked to his car in the parking lot. It was still daylight, but a man wielding a pistol rushed to his car just after he had sat down and demanded that he give him his wallet. The pistol pointed at his head, he handed over his wallet. The suspect left and the shaken man gave himself a few minutes to calm down. He was startled again when this suspect returned with his pistol, but now also had an accomplice that was armed with an Uzi submachine gun (but probably a Tec-9). Now he was ordered to get out of his car, hand over his keys, and then run. He did so, thinking that they were going to shoot him in the back. When he had the courage to return, he of course saw that his car had been stolen by the suspects.

In the early 1990's many Dallas Bingo Halls were being burglarized. They were being targeted randomly without a discernible pattern; police just hoped to get lucky with an arrest.

My partner and I responded to a burglar alarm at a Bingo Hall one night. When we drove up, the alarm was sounding. We quickly drove around the building but saw no one suspicious. Returning to the front we saw a broken windowpane caused by a hurled refrigerator motor, then immediately after noticed a large man standing inside the building with a shotgun at port arms. My first thought was that there was going to be a gun fight, and we were going to be on the receiving end of the heavy artillery. My partner mentioned that this chain of Bingo Parlors had hired armed security guards to thwart the Bingo Burglars. An unknown suspect had broken the window and ran off when the guard appeared from behind the back counter.

Officers can sense nervousness from suspects and often whether the response will be fight or flight. A rookie and I were finishing up with a minor accident, and from the same parking lot I detected the odor of marijuana. I alerted my rookie. Two males had opened their car doors, and we were downwind from them. They had walked into the gas station. When they returned, I asked the driver why the inside of his car smelled like marijuana, and he said that he had some at the house. I opened his driver door and saw a clear baggie of weed tucked between the driver seat and the center console. Sensing a possible uncooperative response, I informed both that the possession of a small quantity of marijuana was just a class B misdemeanor, only one step worse than a ticket, and not to make things any worse than what they were. The driver told his passenger to be cool, and they went to jail for possession of marijuana and ticket warrants respectively.

These two large suspects could have made things difficult for us.

At the start of my shift, I read a short-photocopied article next to the computer that I was using to check my emails. The article stated that 2008 had been a lower than usual year for police officer deaths; 140 nationally, the lowest total since 1966 and a full 30 lower than in 2007. Ironically, several hours later during my shift, a well-respected hard-working Dallas PD Gang Unit Officer became a statistic when he was shot in the face through a door. He was the first officer killed in the USA in 2009.

I had just finished having lunch with two friends from a different patrol division and we were going back to our squad cars when my dispatcher said that there was an "Assist Officer" at the closest intersection to us, which was the patrol division border. We rushed over and the officer who made the request was amazed at our rapid response time. We saw him handcuffing a male and ran to help without yet knowing the circumstances. The arrested male had been drinking and had been argumentative with his wife in the car and the officer, but not with his 21-year-old son who was also present. It seemed the man had been in and out of prison and was just getting to know his son again when this happened, and he knew that he was once again destined for prison. The father wanted to say goodbye to his son, and we allowed this. The son hugged his handcuffed dad, and both were sobbing. Their cries were interspersed with near constant declarations of "I love you dad!" and "I love you son!" ad infinitum. I saw the depressed father just feet away from the bridge rail. Not knowing his thoughts, I lead him further away, lest he decide to take a header to the freeway down below. We separated father and son, and as the son was walking away in the distance, dad shouted one more time (You guessed it) "I love you son!" and his son replied (You guessed it again) "I love you dad!"

A man called 911 to say that he hadn't seen bicycle officers at the lake in a while and wanted to see the blond so that he could pepper spray her. There was only one blond female at the lake, so she had to ride mandatory two-man for several days. If she was alone and he pepper sprayed her, it would've been a deadly force situation; if blinded the suspect could try to kill her and she would then only have one option. The suspect was identified, and a bulletin went out to officers at the NE Patrol Division of his threat. I did some ticket research and saw that the suspect had been ticketed twenty times by officers in just 6 years (underscoring a likely attitude problem). His violations included Traffic, Assault, Littering, and Alcohol in the Park among others. The last officer to issue him a ticket at the lake was one year earlier for Alcohol in the Park. That officer was me. Some officers laughingly speculated that the suspect was still upset over his encounter with me but was projecting his anger toward a much smaller officer.

I had just stopped inside a liquor store and was enjoying my Red Bull Energy drink when a barefooted male walked inside and with an unsteady gait made his way to a beer cooler. There he grabbed three 24 oz. beer cans, then a fifth of whiskey and started to make his way to the counter. I interrupted him and told him to put down the alcohol because he wouldn't be buying any today. He did so, then stepped outside as I asked. He had driven drunk from his home a few miles away (but I never saw him driving).

The crooked-toothed drunkard went to Detox in our Paddy Wagon van.

In early December 2013, rain turned to sleet turned to ice. My day started with me using my fist to hopefully crack the layer of ice around my driver side car door. I gave my door handle a tug, but it was brittle from an upper 20's' temperature, and it came off in my hand. Below was my first call that day.

At work a concerned man called my police station from Houston and asked if someone could do a welfare check on his 90-year-old parents who lived at the lake where I worked and were without power from ice having snapped so many electric lines. I walked up a long sloped icy driveway and when they came to the front door, they were wearing jackets, hats, and gloves. They were staying warm by being huddled around their fireplace, but they were out of firewood with the last logs on the fire. I told them that I could buy them some firewood and asked them what else they might need. She said two cups of coffee would be great. I returned from a slow drive to a 7-Eleven with firewood bundles, having bought the seven that remained unsold, as well as their coffee. It took me five trips up their icy driveway from my car to their fireplace. I spoke with them for just a few minutes after she paid me for the firewood when the power returned. At least they were prepared for the winter in case the power went out again.

They had 4 sons living in Houston and California who were surprised, grateful, and impressed that an officer would take the time like that to help their parents. Actually, when it's that cold in Dallas, our call load slows down considerably, and I was happy to help.

Riding my police bicycle down a winding bike trail, I spied a male walk across the bike trail some 40 yards ahead of us and start to walk up a dirt hill under a DART Rail Track. I saw what appeared to be a can of spray paint in his right hand and told him to come back down to us. My partner noticed the same look on the suspects face and smartly rode up behind him to block any attempt to flee. I confiscated the can of white spray paint in his hand and looked across the trail to view a 3-foot diameter white circle with a capital "A" in it. The paint still smelled fresh, as did the nozzle of the can he had held in his hand. He freely admitted to the graffiti and apologized. We had missed him in the act by several seconds and we could not arrest him. The suspect had been drinking beer, and he had three other spray paint can tops in his small plastic grocery bag he had been carrying: chrome, orange, and red, as well as some more beer. It was DART property, so I summoned their police to do the graffiti report. We released the suspect after we identified him by valid ID. I told him that spray paint can only be purchased by those over 21 because it was thought that at that age, they would be considered old enough to not abuse it. Our suspect was 33. He was a green-haired unemployed mechanic living with Grandma, and tried to make his mark on the world by spray painting the first letter of his first name inside a circle where passersby could see it.

An honest homeless man held a cardboard sign at a median to solicit motorists that read "Why lie? I need $ for a beer!"

A well-dressed man in his twenties stopped by an apartment complex office and kindly inquired about employment but there were no positions available. Two weeks passed and the young man returned and told the lone leasing agent in the office that he really needed a job. Rising from her chair and admiring his dedication for finding a job, she turned around and stooped down to retrieve an application from a file cabinet. Seconds later, she felt the cold steel of a butcher knife blade being held to her throat. The suspect told her that he didn't want to hurt her, but that she needed to give him all her jewelry. She gave him all $2000 of it, which she had foolishly and ostentatiously flashed daily in the office of this low-income apartment complex. He ordered her into a closet on her knees facing away from the door, and she believed that he might slash her throat. He closed the closet door, and she could hear him pulling out desk drawers looking for something valuable to steal. He found her car keys and that became his getaway vehicle.

I was eating Tacos with another uniformed officer when we heard an unknown male from the bar area loudly shout out the F word while watching football on TV. Several parents with their children present stopped what they were doing and looked that way. Moments later I walked over to the bar area and made eye contact with the bartender. I gave her a thumbs up, and she smiled and returned a thumbs up. I went back to sit down and a minute later a drunk male approached us and told us- two uniformed officers- that he wanted to buy us some shots. I told him that we can't accept his offer, but that we appreciated it. He looked perplexed from that answer, so I told him again. He tried to engage us in conversation. I told him to go back and sit down in the bar and wait on his cab (called for him by the bartender), and that he could be arrested for Profanity in Public and Public Intoxication. Still, he lingered. I told him we were trying to finish our dinner and trying to be nice to him, that he needed to go back and sit down. Stupefied, he just wasn't getting it. The other officer told him bluntly that I was telling him to go away. Depressed, he walked over to the bar to wait on his taxi.

The next visit we heard that he was quietly grumbling and bad-mouthing us afterwards.

I arrived at a disturbance call and the suspect started to walk away. He ran away seconds later, but I had a faulty hand-held radio and had to run back to my squad car to broadcast a description. Somehow, he ran across an 8-lane freeway at 11 a.m. without getting hit. A citizen saw him run into a convenience store. Panting and sweating, he was ready to surrender when I arrived.

Saturday morning, I was dispatched to a house where a father had called to report that his kindergarten aged daughter had been sexually molested by her pre-pubescent cousin who had been there visiting. He had done oral sex on her, fingered her, and then had anal sex with her. I handcuffed the boy and placed him in the back seat of my squad car. An officer was going to remain behind because the girl's bedroom was now a crime scene and had to be secured for the arrival of the Physical Evidence Section. The parents had hoped for a quick departure by the police because in just thirty minutes they were expecting people to start arriving for another child's birthday party. This put them in an awkward position of having to provide an explanation as to why police officers were at their house. I told them that they could provide any explanation they wanted, but we couldn't arrive, make an arrest, and process a crime scene in just thirty minutes.

The parents told us that about a year earlier, the 12-year-old suspect's 4-year-old sister had told their parents that he had sexually assaulted her (not in those words of course). The brother had emphatically denied having done anything to his sister, saying that she was just making it up and imagining the whole ordeal. After repeated denials, and not wanting to believe that their own son could do such a thing, they decided to believe him and let it go. Now having raped his young cousin, his earlier molestation allegation was given new credibility.

A young reborn Christian had just finished attending a church service and walked to a bus stop, where three teenaged boys were seated on the bench. The young man decided to strike up a conversation with these three teens and began to tell them about today's Gospel and the bible. One suspect asked him if he was being funny, and the complainant assured him that he was being serious. The three suspects rose to their feet laughing, and one suspect told the complainant that he should give him his shoes, while another suspect told him that he should give him his money. The complainant was now nervous and pulled out his pants packets to reveal that they were empty. Two of the suspects punched the complainant, one blow to his chest and another to his stomach. The complainant backed up and assumed a boxing stance. The suspects all laughed and then punched him again in the stomach, his chest, and one swung a punch to his left temple. When the complainant fell to the ground, the fist strikes became multiple kick strikes as he curled into a protective ball. The suspects all laughed, walked away, turned as if they were returning to give him a scare, only to leave for good. They were not found.

A man was sitting and working at his desk at the rear of his house. His rear door was open for fresh air so his cat could wander in and out of his fenced backyard. A suspect suddenly appeared and pointed a black semi-auto pistol at his head and told him to stand up. The suspect found a wad of $220 in a rubber band in his pants pocket and took it. The suspect began to pull off his wedding ring and watch but the complainant just did it for him. Opening a desk drawer, the suspect saw several bullets and asked where the gun was. The complainant lied and said that his son had it. The suspect ordered the man to lie on the bed and used a belt to tightly bind his hands. The suspect fled in the homeowner's truck, damaging the overhead door as he backed out of the garage. The man twisted his hands until they were bloodied and freed himself with the extra slipperiness. Not wanting to see if the suspect might still be in his house, he ran next door and had a neighbor call police.

A female driver saw a man sitting on a guardrail by a sidewalk, facing the water on the north end of White Rock Lake. It appeared to her that he might jump, so she circled back around after a U-turn. He was no longer there, just his two bags. She called 911, and I was nearly there when the call was read out. The Fire Department was also dispatched. I looked over the rail into a flooded area of the woods below but didn't see any ripples in the water. The Fire Department launched a rubber raft to find him but launched from too far away. I walked down to the riverbank edge to get a better look under the bridge. I stopped, looked, listened, and heard the movement of water. I saw a male walking from the woods in waist deep water, carrying a football. He said he jumped into the murky water because he wanted the football. I was astonished that he hadn't thought about how shallow the water might be, or that he might be jumping onto a submerged stump or branches given the waters' murkiness. I had already looked in his bags and found his wallet with credit cards, a military V.A. Hospital card, and a book about Alcoholics Anonymous. I called to him using his name to make sure he was alright and told him to move to the bank to get back up on the bridge. He said OKAY, but I lost sight of him as he moved through the water into a more heavily foliaged area. I thought that he might be looking for a sloped shoreline area where it was easier to get to me. Minutes later, it was obvious that he was avoiding me when the fire department said they had a male swimming in the water. I searched and could now see that the man was swimming away from the woods and into the lake. The two-man fire rescue boat motored out to him, but he didn't want to be rescued and pushed away. I was a little agitated that the firemen were reluctant to grab him, and just reported his whereabouts on the radio. I drove over to the dog park where I correctly predicted he would be coming ashore. I confronted him as he walked toward me dripping wet and ordered him to drop the concrete chunks that he held in each of his fists, then I handcuffed him. He was still carrying the football he had found in the water. At first, he answered my questions, but then said that he didn't want to talk. After the paramedics did a cursory check, I took him to a psychiatric hospital. I believed that he was a veteran of Iraq or Afghanistan and suffered from PTSD.

A man that had been loitering outside a business for about 10 minutes stepped inside and looked around for about 10 minutes more. The store manager recognized him as having visited just a couple of days earlier. The man stepped behind the manager then struck him on his forehead twice with an unknown object, causing the manager to fall to the floor. The suspect demanded that the manager give him his wallet, which he did, then told him to get up and open the register. In total the manager gave up about $150, then laid back on the floor as instructed. Though the suspect warned him to lay down for 30 minutes and not move or he'd kill him, the manager locked the front door after the suspect had left and then called police. I arrived to see a bloody-faced manager holding what was now a mostly red rag on his forehead. I broadcasted a suspect description and within minutes an officer found him a few blocks away. He was returned to the store where the manager identified him as the Aggravated Robbery Suspect, and his wallet, cash, and cell phone were returned to him. A paramedic treated the gash on the forehead of the manager.

The suspect commented that he had been in prison for too long and he couldn't function outside prison in the real world; he'd been institutionalized. His commission of this crime assured him of another prison term where he felt at peace and at home.

I had arrested a man for DWI after stopping him for failing to maintain a single lane of traffic. He had failed all sobriety tests, and at about 2:30 a.m. when he took the breathalyzer test at the county jail, he blew .16 on two successive readings (twice the legal DWI limit of .08 BAC, or Blood Alcohol Concentration).

Months later at his trial he was being defended by a good, well-known Defense Attorney. Her strategy was to cause doubt in my mind as to whether I was misremembering and confusing her client with one of my other DWI arrests. I had only been an officer for several years at this point, worked the day shift, and usually only had a DWI arrest if I worked overtime as part of a task force. She inquired how many arrests for DWI I had made in my career. I had no idea but may have guessed too high. If she knew that number from an open record request, she never corrected me. She asked me how it was that I could remember her client and distinguish him from all my other DWI arrests. I replied because of what he said to me on the way to jail and at the jail, leading her to her next question of what he had said to me on the way to jail. I answered that he was nervous and worried because he had never been to jail before and wanted to know what was going to happen. She liked that answer, with my having told the jury that her client had never been to jail. She then asked what he said to me at the jail, hoping to get more positive feedback about her client that made him out to be a good man. It backfired. I replied "He told me that, --what did I make last year--, $30,000? That he made over $100,000. That he paid my salary. That physically I was a big man, but I was really just a little man in a big man's uniform. When somebody insults and humiliates me, I remember those arrests. I remember those arrests very well." Now the defense attorney had a shocked look across her face, not having expected my testimony to portray her client as a pompous, arrogant rich man. Dismissed from testifying shortly thereafter, I waited in the District Attorney workroom. When the trial recessed, the Defense Attorney stepped out and glared at me for several seconds from the workroom doorway.

Her client was quickly found guilty in a short sequestering of the jury.

I had the occasion one fall semester to instruct two 6th grade classes as a L.E.T.S. Instructor (Law Enforcement Teaching Students). Once a week for each class I would teach a lesson for a total of six weeks covering subjects like self-empowerment, making good decisions, helpful resources and agencies and when to call the police, and the need to resist peer pressure to avoid the dangers associated with it—drugs, gangs, cigarettes, and alcohol.

I attended a three-day class with the Dallas P.D. to teach the L.E.T.S. curriculum. A few current instructors spoke to us, and one of them said that once after a class, one of his students told him that she had been raped. None of the officers in the class believed that a situation like that could arise in any of their classes. I mean, really, what were the odds of that happening?

As a L.E.T.S. instructor, each of our classrooms had a shoebox in which students could drop questions about law enforcement for us to answer. On my very first day I was pulling out questions that the students had written on a scrap of paper. I enjoyed answering the questions and everything was going just fine. Then I pulled out a torn piece of paper that contained three questions: "1) Have you ever shot anybody (the most common question) 2). Have you ever put a gun to someone's head? 3). I have been raped. Can you arrest him and put him in jail? Please help Me!" She signed it with her name. I didn't read her final question aloud. When the class was over, the victimized 13-year-old approached me and meekly said that she needed to talk to me. I spoke to a member of the Administration office and was shown a small room with windows across the hall where we could speak privately. There I discovered that from the day after her eleventh birthday, an aunt's boyfriend had raped her by her own estimate forty times a year. Many times, when the aunt was asleep the child molester would prowl into her bedroom and never say a word while he sexually violated her. The girl told her aunt who at first believed her, but after repeated denials the rapist convinced the aunt that the girl's repeated allegations were the result of her vivid imagination and that he never touched her. Inexcusably, the aunt believed (probably wanted to believe) him. The rapes continued.

I made several phone calls, and determined that a report had already been made two weeks earlier. The investigative process was already underway. The victim had made an outcry to a teacher, who reported it to a school counselor, who contacted the Department of Family Services. The girl told me that she had spoken to a man in a suit, but that she didn't believe that he was a policeman. I assured her that that man was a detective and that he was a police officer. She didn't see a police uniform and didn't know that the police were even involved. I emphasized to her that everything was on track and going well.

I supplemented the original Offense report with my situation to help prosecute the case and placed the scrap of paper with the girl's questions in the property room as evidence.

I stopped a motorist and while talking to him noticed that I couldn't see his left leg. He was skinny, and so I thought that he just had a skinny leg, or perhaps I wasn't standing close enough to the door to see his left side. I checked his DL on my computer and found some traffic ticket warrants that I confirmed as valid. I returned to the man's vehicle and informed him that he was being arrested for unpaid tickets. I opened the driver door and then realized why I didn't see his left leg; he didn't have one! I carefully stood him against the car after I handcuffed him for his search. I supported his left arm as he hopped back to the police car. I got him a wheelchair at the City Detention Center.

The story of the missing limb? A man had shot him in the left leg with a 12-gauge shotgun. For whatever reason, he never sought medical attention. His leg became infected and gangrenous and had to be amputated. The same man used the same shotgun to shoot another man in the back and then went to prison. The shooter on both occasions was his own brother.

On a Saturday morning, a 17-year-old gang member drove his pickup truck onto a front lawn and started blasting his horn. He had met a guy at a party, and that young man lived there. The new friend woke up and stepped outside to talk to the driver, who was drunk and holding a can of beer in his hand. The drunken gang banger said "C'mon man! You got some beer? Let's party!" Two other gang members were also in the truck. The kid who stepped outside told him that it was too early to drink, and that they needed to get off the front lawn because his parents spend a lot of money on it. Shouting a few epithets and unable to relate to a good kid, the gang members left. Undeterred, they called back a little later and said they were coming over. The kid told them that they can't come over. The now angry driver told him they'd be coming over to shoot up his house. Thirty minutes later they returned for a drive by and fired a barrage of pistol shots, but no bullet holes were found. Several neighbors in the area called 911 about having heard gun shots.

A billiards hall bartender called police to get a drunk off the premises. They noticed that he was a bit too inebriated and should go home, so they did the right thing and put him in a cab for a ride home at their expense. The drunk instead had the cab driver take him back to the billiards hall because he wasn't finished drinking yet. Bad decisions have consequences. We rewarded his poor judgment by taking him to Detox.

Two brothers, 5 and 9, walked a ½ mile in mid-nineties heat to go to a City Recreation Center. After 5 hours of being unsupervised, a coach phoned 911. The boys told me that their teenaged sister was usually responsible for watching them, but she wasn't even in the apartment when they woke up. They thought she was probably at a friend's apartment, and that turned out to be true. I phoned her and she was unconcerned about their whereabouts, saying that they were probably playing basketball. She only became concerned for their welfare after I identified myself as a police officer on the phone. The mother of all was contacted at work and came home to take custody of them.

I was taking an Aggravated Robbery report while outside talking to the complainant. The complainant noticed a passing vehicle and told me that he believed the driver to be the suspect that robbed him yesterday. I quickly entered my vehicle and made a traffic stop on the suspect when a cover officer arrived behind me. I had the driver exit his car at gunpoint and patted him down for weapons after I handcuffed him. He kept trying to lean forcefully against his vehicle to prevent me from searching his front two-sided sweatshirt pocket. He had two crystal blue baggies of marijuana.

We returned the suspect to the scene, and after a viewing, the robbery complainant ended up stating that this man was not the suspect that had robbed him the day before. Legally, I had acted without malice and any reasonable officer would have done the same. The wrong place/wrong time motorist went to jail for marijuana possession.

I stopped a man on a Sunday morning for a traffic violation. He didn't have a DL so he verbally gave me his name, DOB, and TX ID card number. I was surprised a computer subject check revealed that same name and birthday came back as an alias name used by a murderer who had a murder warrant out of Dodge City, KS. Rather than waste precious time wading through the computer details and possibly having a dangerous, volatile situation, for my safety I asked the dispatcher to send me some cover. Two officers arrived, and I reapproached the driver. It turned out that the actual murder suspect had somehow stolen this man's identity, though the height and weight were notably different. I didn't have a murder suspect, but I did have a man who had violated a Protective Order. He was supposed to stay away from the complainant, but she was seated next to him in the car. I arrested him for that violation of an active Protective Order but found out later that a Judge had released him. It seemed the P.O. stipulated that he had to be at least 500 feet away from her workplace and her home, but it was legal for him to be seated next to her in the same car, if it was further than 500 feet from both places. How asinine.

Having handled a call, we were already on the complex property and walking out when a manager informed us that a woman who had previously received a Criminal Trespass

Warning was back on the property. The manager gave us the apartment number of where the woman was believed to be visiting, and we all walked over. The tenant told us that the woman was not in his apartment. Suspecting otherwise, the manager asked him if we could go inside and look. The tenant agreed, telling us that we can look but we weren't going to find her because she wasn't there. I found the woman standing naked and trying to hide inside his bedroom closet. She went to jail for Criminal Trespassing.

Apparently, there are men who will lie to the police to keep a naked woman in their apartment.

A motorist was stopped for an expired registration and an RGN (Regional) "hit", (this one with ticket warrants attached to his vehicle). The driver told me his name but said that he didn't have any ID on him. I had him step out of his car and I could see that he did not have a wallet in his pants pocket. I told him to sit back down and said that if he was lying to me about his name that it would be an additional charge of Failure to ID as a Fugitive if he had any warrants including ticket warrants. He assured me that he wasn't lying. I couldn't find any ID under the name and DOB that he gave me, but I did find two ticket warrants under the name that he gave me (which turned out to be an alias name that he used to give police). I wrote him a citation for the expired registration, and he signed it. I gave him his copies and walked back to my squad car. Now I noticed that by force of habit, he had signed the citation with his true name, the one with multiple warrants, and he didn't sign with the name that he told me. I quickly pulled him over again after he'd only gone twenty yards, and he was arrested for over a dozen ticket warrants and the Failure to ID as a Fugitive charge.

A bank manager had recently told his tellers to be more wary of checks from strangers as there had been many check forgeries at other bank branches recently. A teller soon alerted her supervisor to a suspicious check that had been presented to her. The check owner was contacted and stated that that check along with many other checks and property had been stolen from her in a recent burglary. After calling the police, I was the first officer on the scene, and I cuffed the 18 -year-old female suspect. Bank employees mentioned that the suspect had stepped out of one of two vehicles that had arrived together and were waiting for her. They wasted no time and drove off as soon as they spotted my arriving police car, leaving the forgery suspect stranded at the bank. Because of attentive bank employees, I quickly broadcasted a description of these two suspect vehicles including their license plate info and miraculously both were stopped by observant officers. All the 4 other suspects had warrants and were transported to our Investigative unit for questioning about the burglary. Because of my time-consuming Forgery arrest, I never did find out if some or all of the other suspects confessed to the burglary.

A teenage boy came to a woman's front door and asked for her son. She didn't know the boy, so she told him that her son wasn't going outside. Minutes later, two neighbors noticed the boy enter the woman's fenced backyard, then pick up and steal her 8-week-old Rottweiler puppy. This boy was then seen walking down the alley with another boy. Another neighbor further down the alley was in his backyard doing yardwork when he watched the boy put the puppy inside a large black plastic trash can, then they both ran off. I arrived at this house to find the dog owner and two witnesses waiting at the front of the house in one car. The unknown teen puppy thief was just visiting the house and was issued a M/C citation for Theft. The dognapped puppy which was now in that house was returned unharmed to the grateful owner.

A woman went to a medical care facility for an exam, and her boyfriend waited for her in the private room where she started. She returned with a doctor who brought him unpleasant news.

The boyfriend became enraged, and madly yelled and shouted. He slammed his palm on the wall and then slapped his girlfriend and shoved her against a wall. Her ear was somehow lacerated in the assault. He left and stormed through the crowded waiting room, slandering his girlfriend as he did. His profanity didn't stop until he entered his car and drove away.

Minutes later I arrived and was led to the woman's waiting room. She was crying and shocked at her boyfriend's outrage but would not identify him as she held a gauze bandage to her bleeding ear. She related that he was moving out of state anyway, and she didn't want to get him in trouble, especially since he had never been violent toward her. I informed her that I needed some facts for my report but that I didn't need his name. She was silent and refused to elaborate. Hidden from her view, a kindly nurse muttered that the boyfriend launched into a tirade because he learned that his girlfriend had the "clap", or gonorrhea, which explained the pus-like discharges he was having from his penis.

The driver of a pickup truck was driving too fast and lost control of the vehicle, jumping a curb and coming to a halt on somebody's front lawn. He and his girlfriend jumped out of the truck and ran across a field. Officers arrived at the location and a 12-year-old boy pointed out where the woman had tossed a pistol to the ground. The weapon was recovered, and the search began in earnest for the missing couple. They were last seen on a RR track walking north. After a twenty-minute search from their police cruisers, most officers abandoned their search efforts and returned to the station; it was close to quitting time. I decided that there may have been a good chance that no officer had left the warmth of their car for a long search on foot. I parked my car, walked through the woods, and walked up a hill with a RR track on top. I walked down the track a distance and stopped to look and listen. I continued walking, then halted and did the same thing again. This time I heard voices. I walked further and looked to my left and saw the suspects at the base of the RR track embankment, just inside a wooded area. When I told them to come on out, they noticed me standing up the incline from them. The woman responded that the man was hurt really bad and that he needed help. I told them to stay put. I descended down the slope and did battle with a maze of thorny vines to reach them. He had a large gash on top of his head and a cut on his forehead. Like a typical head laceration, it looked worse that it was, and his hair was a bloody matted mess. His T-shirt didn't have a strange red printed design as I had originally thought, but rather blood drop stains from his head wound. I handcuffed him and ordered her to walk in front of us. She complained of shoulder and clavicle pain and tried to persuade me to just let them go. Both were intoxicated. I informed the dispatcher that both accident suspects were in my custody and requested an ambulance for them. We arrived back to the parking lot where I had left my car, and a short time later an ambulance arrived and whisked them away. Had they remained, the only charge would've been Public Intoxication. No charges were filed against them because there was no lawn damage, and the only witness who saw the drunken man driving and the female toss the gun was the 12-year-old boy. However, their action would not escape un-noticed, as having slammed into the curb had made his employer company truck un-drivable. It was towed to our Auto Pound, and the spilled load of PVC pipe that had broken free and was strewn about the lawn was being retrieved by one of his coworkers. Drinking and driving during work hours would surely cost him his job.

A couple phoned the police because intermittently for the previous few weeks, someone had tossed feces in toilet paper over their privacy fence into their backyard. They wondered how anybody walking down their alley could fling excrement loaded toilet paper over their tall wooden privacy fence and have it land at the same spot next to the privacy fence adjacent to a neighbor. I agreed with them that the evidence didn't appear to have been picked up but rather wiped. They didn't want to point fingers but mentioned that two older brothers lived next door, and one of them seemed a bit off at times. I told them that I would simply talk to them to see what they knew and not hurl any accusations.

I took my rookie to the house next door and knocked, only to find the door ajar. The door opened more as I knocked (the doorbell didn't work). We entered the house to check on the welfare of the aged siblings and announced "DALLAS POLICE" often as we did so, downstairs and upstairs. No one was home, so we locked and closed the front door upon our exit. Walking back toward their garage, we could hear music from within. I knocked and the door was opened from within by one of the brothers. Immediately scenting the smell of burning marijuana, I pushed the door open and asked who had been smoking it. The other brother was present inside. No response from either of them. I looked around the crowded garage and atop a card table loaded with many small items, I plucked two baggies of marijuana and inquired as to who owned it. Again, silence. I added they both lived there and so I supposed that we would be arresting both of them. One brother took the fall whether it belonged to him or not and declared that the marijuana was his own. He was handcuffed. Seconds later, the other brother (the slow one) reached over to the trinket-strewn card table and selected a large, folded pocketknife and put his other hand on the folded blade to open it, asking "Is this knife legal?" I quickly snatched the unopened knife from his hands and angrily asked what he was doing, that I had just arrested his brother and I was supposed to let him open a large knife in front of us? He looked puzzled and told us that he didn't mean nothing by it.

The brother that we arrested had last been arrested decades before and did time in prison for having been in possession of a much larger quantity of marijuana. While we were at jail, the remaining brother kept calling 911 to threaten the police and said we arrested the wrong brother, that the cops better not ever come to the house again. Several police officers went to the house for his making abusive 911 calls. He wasn't nearly so agitated in person as he was over the phone, and received a citation, being told to stop abusing 911. The house address was flagged for officers' safety for future 911 calls by being made a "Hazardous Address."

Before we left for jail, I had asked the brother if they had a bathroom. It was shown to us, and we were told that the toilet didn't work. The bathroom window was next to the neighbor's privacy fence. I told the slow brother that if the toilet didn't work, then he needed to stop using it, and to stop throwing toilet paper out of the window. He looked baffled that I knew so much.

We went to an apartment with a woman who had stated that one of the four men inside had committed a simple assault against her. They had all been smoking crack cocaine earlier that day. No one inside replied to repeated door knocks and all was quiet. No keyholder was available to unlock the door. As we were about to leave, our complainant mentioned that a woman seen loitering in the complex courtyard was the ex-girlfriend of the man who assaulted her. We decided to question her about his whereabouts so that we could issue an assault citation and clear the offense. She covered for him and just said she knew him only by "D" which we already knew. I asked her name, and she told her name and her birthday. I did a computer check on her and found a woman with a different first name and a DOB exactly one year off that had a probation violation out of Dallas County. Conveniently for our suspect, she had no purse with her ID because it had been stolen. She was from Illinois originally. I asked for her birthday again, and she gave me another birth year one year over the first one she had given me. I didn't want to chance releasing a subject with a probation violation, so we cuffed her and took her to be fingerprinted. She had no arrest record in Dallas County. She said she understood the situation and actually appreciated our diligence.

On the return to her apartment complex, we stopped at a KFC drive thru to buy her a lunch for the inconvenience, as she was a very nice lady caught up in exigent circumstances.

We went to a door on the third floor to locate our complainant who had reported that she had tried to exit a man's apartment, but he had pulled her back inside with a pistol in his other hand. I was uncomfortable knocking on the front door, not just because I could be shot through the door but also because there was an apartment window behind me for an ambush. The other officer stood several steps down the stairwell for an interior view of the apartment when the door opened. Somewhere in the distance outside an unknown male yelled "FUCK THE POLICE!" No one was seen. I knocked on the door and again from outside the same voice was heard to say, "FUCK THE POLICE!" The door opened and the male was wearing a blanket as if he had just awakened. We explained our purpose, but he was alone and said we could check to see for ourselves. We did, and he was alone.

We left and decided to search for the irreverent miscreant who had insulted us and to write him a citation for Disorderly Conduct, Profanity in Public if we could find a witness, but all was quiet.

A drunken woman was living out of her truck and was probably a prostitute. She got into a verbal altercation with a man over an unknown cause. Provoked, she stepped out of her truck after placing it in neutral. It was stopped behind a very low curb. As she was at the rear of her truck, the man lurched up with his vehicle and tightly pinned her between bumpers. She was not hurt or in pain, so she wiggled herself free. In doing so, she pushed her truck over the low curb, and it rolled down the slight descending parking lot, jumped a parking space curb and crashed a gaping hole into a pizza chain restaurant picture window. The drunken woman sauntered down to her truck, entered, and reversed back over the curb and into a parking space, being seen by several witnesses who had also seen her drive into the parking lot from the street. We arrived and she was arrested for DWI. It bothered me that she had a "USMC" tattoo on one ankle. She was seen by a nurse at jail because she had 19 prescription medicine bottles in her purse.

A 74-year-old man invited a 30ish woman that he knew to be a prostitute to come into his apartment. No sex occurred, but the man admitted liking the woman's mannerisms and attention. They had a beer or two, and then the woman departed. Soon the man realized that $38 was missing from atop his microwave.

Four days passed and the woman returned. The geriatric male opened the door and the woman slipped inside. He told her to leave because she stole money from him on her last visit, but she denied it. She smiled and put her hand into his right pants pocket and began playing with and stroking his penis from inside the pocket. The man eventually told her to stop that and to get out. She pulled her hand out of his pocket, along with the $7 he had in there, and once again left with some of his money.

A driver at the lake would not pass a couple of bicyclists. The motorist behind him became impatient and tried to pass, but the car in front wouldn't allow it. The second vehicle finally did pass, but clipped the left rear of the car as he did. The vehicle he had struck was now behind him, following because he wasn't stopping from the minor accident. He phoned 911 and some nearby officers stopped the vehicle. The driver had no DL, no insurance, and an expired license plate, and received those citations. He was no stranger to law enforcement, having been arrested for Aggravated Sexual Assault, Indecency with a Child, Evading, and Robbery, among others. The car was towed for no insurance. He exchanged info with the other driver involved in the minor accident. I asked the ex-con who the two women were in his car. He replied that they were "my ladies, and they work for me to make me money." They showed no surprise when an officer relayed that comment to them. I had the two women step into the back seat of my squad car but told the ex-con that there was no room for him (given the width of one of his "ladies", there really wasn't). He didn't like me and instead of looking at my name tag he wrote down my car number and was going to call his lawyer. Another officer offered to give him a ride to the same 7-Eleven where his ladies were going to be dropped off, but he bluntly and angrily retorted that he wasn't getting into the back seat of a police car (bad memories) and began walking.

A female homeowner watched as a strange man knocked on her front door with his knuckles, his head, and sometimes his feet. The woman phoned police because he wasn't going away, and she was scared. I arrived to find the young man at an adjacent house and pulled into that driveway. As I did, he stepped off the porch and started walking toward me. I had him stop and patted him down for my safety, but all his pockets were empty. The man explained that his beater corvette had run out of gas, and as it sputtered to a stop, he drove into the woman's driveway rather than steer to the street curb. He was going to ask people if they could spare a few bucks for gasoline. The first homeowner told me that she had observed him through her peep hole with his head turned and talking, and she first thought that someone was with him. She soon realized that he was alone and talking to himself. Soon after, she peeked again but didn't see him. However, the front porch motion sensor light was still lit so she worried that he may still be present. After she had phoned police, she again peered into her peephole and last saw him running both of his palms downward over his face just like actor Curly of The Three Stooges. That is when she realized that he had mental issues. He hadn't ingested his bi-polar/schizophrenia meds for two days and had been living out of his car. I had an officer watch him while I went to get him a few bucks worth of gas for his mobile home, then returned and gave him $2 to send him on his way, reminding him to take his medication.

I could see a vehicle up ahead increasing its distance from me, and I sped up to the speeding vehicle and paced him driving 55 mph in a 35-mph zone. I flipped on my emergency lights switch, but the motorist did not stop. A few blocks later, the motorist turned down a side street and quickly came to a halt in front of his house. I couldn't mark out on a traffic stop because of too much radio chatter from another police situation. I didn't have time to switch to a different channel to mark out because my suspect was now stepping out of his vehicle. I intercepted him as he was already walking toward his house and told him that I needed to see his DL and proof of financial responsibility (insurance). He asked, "For what?" I told him for speeding. He denied speeding and asked to see my "clock". I paced him at that speed and didn't have a clock and told him that I didn't have to show him. I reiterated that I needed to see his DL and insurance. "I don't have time for this shit! I need to go to work!" then continued walking to his front door saying that he needed to give his wife the keys. I lurched forward and reminded him that he was being lawfully detained, that he needed to stop, and he wasn't free to walk away. He ignored me and kept walking. I grabbed his sweaty right arm and did a straight arm bar take down maneuver, taking him to the ground of his front yard and told him that he was going to jail. He slipped from my grasp and walked inside his house with me directly behind him. I now had my mace in one hand and could see a few children. I told the suspect that he needed to step outside, or I would mace him in front of his kids. He tossed his keys to his wife, and after some hesitation stepped outdoors. I retrieved my police radio which had unknowingly fallen to the grass in the brief scuffle, then requested cover. I told the suspect that he still needed to show me his ID. He replied that he had ticket warrants, and he would not go to jail because he would not lose his job over this. Two officers arrived and I handcuffed him under their watchful eyes. His wife brought me his ID, and I took him to jail for Evading Detention and his two ticket warrants.

Along the way, the arrestee shook his head and exhibited some introspection and self-reflection when he commented "That's my problem, I always have to do what I want to do. All I had to do was listen."

The irony was that I was enroute to meet two friends for lunch at the time I initiated contact with this suspect. He may have received a speeding ticket, but I would have given him a warning to take care of his two tickets warrants so as to not be late. All he had to do was be cooperative, as he said.

A woman was despondent and distraught because someone had betrayed her trust and stolen $10,000. She sent text messages to a friend saying that she was ready to end it all, was tired of everything, and was loading bullets into her Ruger pistol. Her friend quickly called the police. Dispatched as a Suicide in progress, I was swift to arrive. When the other officer arrived, we knocked on the door with pistols pointed down by our side and announced "Police!" The woman opened the door for us, and we stepped inside. I made a serpentine around her and scanned her apartment looking for the pistol after inquiring about it. I did the same upstairs. The woman became agitated and didn't like my meandering about her apartment and told us to get out. I told her that we would not be leaving until we determined that she wasn't going to hurt herself. Two other officers arrived. Full of despair, she said aloud that she was "Pissed, angry, depressed, and suicidal." That last one did it for all of us, and I told her to put her hands behind her back. She didn't readily want to do that denying that she had said "suicidal". She cried while going to the Psychiatric Hospital, saying that this went to her character and might make her ineligible to take the Texas Bar Exam three months from then.

Her friend told me by phone that the woman was possibly bipolar given her mood swings and might be abusing her prescription drugs.

I stopped a male for warrant hits on a vehicle registration check. He told me that he had a DL but it wasn't with him. I wrote down his name and DOB, then checked him on my computer. I couldn't find a DL with his name, but I did find some ticket warrants with his info. I wrote him a ticket and decided to overlook his two ticket warrants for his arrest. He signed the ticket with his first name spelled differently than the common spelling. The traffic stop was over, so I returned to my car and the motorist drove away. I only had to turn in the top or green copy of every ticket, so I would just use some "green-out" to make the correction on that green copy. I now checked his name with the correct spelling of his first name and now I found a DL that belonged to him, and noticed that it had been suspended. He was already gone, so he avoided an arrest for Driving While License Suspended. I was able to verify that his identity was correct because I checked with the county jail, and they sent me a picture from his arrest record. For the first time in 12 years--and the only time in my career-- I filed a DWLS case at large.

A bicyclist flagged me down about an older silver Cadillac that had been parked for hours at the lake with 3 people in it. I had seen the vehicle earlier and had already checked the registration. I circled back and found a father, mother, and their 4-year-old daughter in the vehicle, along with a little brown dog curled up on the back seat sleeping. I asked if they were homeless because their car was messy with refuse, and they had been at the lake for 6 hours at this point. The young man said they had been waiting for 3 hours for a friend to drive up from a southern suburb. They lived 2.5 miles away and the man could've walked that in an hour, but he told his wife that he didn't want to walk that far. I was stunned that they'd been there 6 hours and accomplished absolutely nothing. I told the wife that I would take her and her daughter home while he waited, and they entered my car carrying their pooch. Arriving at their house, there was a small, playful young puppy on their front lawn. It had to belong to one of their neighbors because it was so young. I suggested placing a few notices on telephone poles to locate the owner. She said she'd use Craigslist because she had used them before; I didn't want to give her a lesson in logic. She could only assemble $3 for gas, which we put into a milk jug for the return.

Conversing with her, I realized that she had been dealt an unlucky hand when it came to her biological parents. She said she was adopted at 13 to good parents but had residual psychological issues stemming from her birth parents. Her real dad was a drug dealer, and her real mom was addicted to crack cocaine. Her real mom once allowed 5 men to have sex with her to get money so she could buy more crack. She was 9 years old at that time, old enough to know and remember what was happening, but powerless to do anything about it. How do you recover from something like that?

We arrived back at the lake and of course the man was unmoved and still waiting for his "friend".

A fellow lake officer checked a registration at night and the vehicle data indicated that the missing front license plate was one of the property items that had been stolen at gunpoint during an Aggravated Robbery. Though it could have belonged to the complainant, the presumption that this vehicle was being driven by the suspect must be made for caution and officer safety. This officer sent me a message to cover him. I was already heading that way when the dispatcher broadcasted the alert that appeared on her screen. When enough officers were present, a traffic stop was made, and officer pistols and AR-15 rifles were deployed from about 10 officers that participated in the suspect takedown at a gas station. The driver was ordered to exit the car and he sprawled out on the pavement. I ordered the female to keep her hands up as she emerged from the vehicle, and I was bewildered that she had a smile on her face and even spun a single circle dance before she lay down on the concrete. The extracted male was the car owner who had made the original report. I explained to her that her boyfriend needed to get new license plates issued to his vehicle and told him where to go and to bring his report so that they could see one of his plates had been stolen. The girl said that he knew about that but had neglected to do that; this was their third time being stopped at gunpoint by the police, which explained her amusement. His procrastination was wasting police efforts and resources.

A woman was on her balcony when she heard a child crying "Mommy". She walked toward the cries and found a 4-year-old crying behind a building near the playground. She had seen the child out there at 7 a.m. unsupervised, and it was now 9 a.m. The little boy led her to his apartment where he left the rear door open, but no one was home. I arrived after she had called the police, but by this time the mother had returned. I asked her where she had been, and she lied and told me she had just been in the parking lot for ten minutes. The good neighbor who had come to the boy's rescue told me that she saw him at the playground most all day every day and he was always alone. I did a CPS referral report.

I was dispatched on a welfare check of an 81-year-old female who had not been seen in six days. A manager was waiting for me at the apartment, and explained to me that the woman was very frail and didn't like to use her air conditioning to save money, despite more than a week of temperatures topping 100 degrees. The manager had unlocked the elderly tenant's front door and stuck his head inside calling her by name. When there was no reply, he phoned police. Things were not looking good. I entered the apartment and detected a slightly pungent odor, but not overpowering. No sign of her on the newspaper covered first floor. I walked upstairs, expecting the odor to become worse. The manager told me that the resident had a dog, but when I inquired, he wasn't sure if it was friendly. I lifted my can of mace to be ready for a charging protective dog. Dogs have been known to eat parts of their deceased master when trapped inside without food. I reached the top of the stairs and could now see a pale, ashen white, scrawny woman lying backwards on her bed in a silken nightgown or negligee. I heard a dog whimper and saw the dog crawl out from under the bed, limping as he did. I thought that the poor dog was weak from hunger. The woman was certainly dead, but I thought I would touch her presumably cold, rigor mortis body to verify lifelessness. As I moved toward her, I was startled by a twitch from one of her fingers. I said aloud "Ma'am, are you okay?" She awakened and eyed me standing there and asked me what was wrong. I told her why I was there. She asked me the time and added that she had overslept.

The manager and neighbors that had gathered outside were relieved when I told them the good news.

A burglary had just occurred, and the suspect was still nearby. Enroute to the call, I spotted a suspect matching the description, red shirt and blue shorts. Knowing that other officers were directly behind me and shrinking the distance quickly, I exited my vehicle and ordered the suspect to place his hands on my hood. He complied. As I began to frisk the suspect, he darted to one side and tried to run, declaring that he couldn't go to jail. I stepped sideways to follow him and after just a few steps grabbed him by his shirt and pulled him down to the grass. The other two officers scurried from their arriving cars to assist me in effecting the arrest. The suspect had a black .38 snub nose revolver in his front left pants pocket, loaded with 5 rounds in the cylinder. The suspect said that he didn't burglarize any house and had put on a white shirt first but switched to a red one because it was clean and just out of the dryer. He carried the gun for protection but had also served prison time for murder. As such, he was also charged with Felon in Possession of Firearm.

This case went to Federal Court where he was convicted with my testimony.

At 9 a.m. a complainant heard some knocks on her door, but she wasn't expecting anyone, so she ignored the knocks and stayed in bed. Minutes later, she heard some unusual noises coming from her apartment, so she got out of bed and walked around a corner. As she did, she came face-to-face with an unknown male. She screamed, and the male quickly ran out the front door. Another officer saw a male fitting the intruder description nearby. I brought the woman to the location, and she positively identified the male.

After no one had come to the door, the suspect incorrectly assumed that no one was home, and climbed up to the second-floor balcony and lifted the patio door from its' track to slide it open. Because no property was stolen, the suspect was arrested for Criminal Trespassing and not Burglary.

Several calls came in about a middle-aged woman who was walking around wearing nothing but her T-backed lacy white panties. I found her and approached as she walked toward me. I was astounded when she asked, "Is something wrong officer?" She had just crossed a six-lane road nearly naked at 1 p.m. She seemed lucid at first until she told me that she was the wife of God and had no home to answer my question because she lived everywhere. A kindly Samaritan provided a robe for her to put on before we handcuffed her. Our Meth user informed us that she was convinced that a certain man was God, but he kept throwing her out of their apartment.

She once again became a psychiatric patient at a familiar hospital.

It was December 23, and I drove to a liquor store near my beat to wish a friend Merry Christmas. I was leaving for Chicago the next day, so it was supposed to be a short visit. My friend handed me a set of van keys and a $20 bill and asked me to do him a favor. A man had walked into the store a short time before and given him those things, explaining that he was tired of dealing with his inebriated girlfriend and was going to take the train home. The money was for a cab driver to bring her home, and when he delivered her, the cabbie would then give her the keys. Seemed simple, but it required her cooperation. She was repeatedly emphatic that she didn't need a ride home and she was comfortable sitting in the van, she didn't want to take a cab. It didn't matter to her that the ride fare had been prepaid. She finally stepped out after she was given the option of taking a cab ride home or getting arrested for Public Intoxication. She entered the cab, and the cabbie was given the $20. I thought the matter was closed, so I began to walk away. The cabbie alerted me that she didn't want to give him her address. Perturbed, I returned and told her to provide him with her address. She said that she didn't remember, and she didn't want a ride home anyway, and proceeded to step out of the cab. I didn't give her a chance to enter the van and cuffed her amid her profanity laced protest to take her to Detox. I now fully understood why her boyfriend had become so intolerant of her and had to get away from her.

A Loss Prevention Officer at an Electronics store followed a 28-year-old male while inside the store because the male was holding his arms at his sides and wasn't swinging them when he walked, postulating that he could have been holding stolen property under his arms. The employee followed the male into the restroom and interrupted the male as he was trying to duct tape 8 music CDs to his ankles under his baggie bottomed pantlegs. Two of the CD's had been under each armpit, and four more had been hidden under his shirt. As the thief was being brought to the office, he tossed the duct tape into the garbage. He had been in the store just 20 minutes earlier and made off with 8 other music CDs, but Loss Prevention had lost him and didn't know that he had exited the store and put those stolen CDs on his car floorboard. Those CDs were recovered and returned. After the first theft, the thief had a cigarette, then returned to the store because it had been so easy. He was oblivious that he was being surveilled. On the way to jail, he stated that he wanted to get some Christmas gifts but didn't have any money. At 350 lbs., it was difficult for him to move comfortably so I doubted that he had made much effort to seek employment.

Stepping outside of his apartment, a man walked to the stairwell and noticed down below in the parking lot that his friends' vehicle had its' driver door open. A male was leaning over the driver seat and searching under it using sweeping motions with his left hand. The man shouted "Hey!" and the culprit ran. I arrived several minutes later and observed that a male ran in front of me. Several helpful people informed me that he was the suspect, relentlessly tugging on many car doors to see if they were unlocked to steal whatever he could find. He had run upstairs and was inside his apartment, and a helpful tenant pointed out his residence. I spoke with his parents who were unsurprised, and they added that he didn't listen and was wild and unruly. They quietly told me that he needed to be taught a valuable, life-changing lesson and taken to jail, though I'd already handcuffed their son. They told their son to do as I said and listen to me. The boy shed some tears but was very respectful and responded with "Yes Sir' and "No sir" whenever I spoke with him. This 10-year-old boy was supposedly a straight "A" student (according to him). He had never been arrested before, so I had told his parents to leave for our Youth Division an hour after we left to reunite with their son. They had hoped his regrettable experience would give him a newfound respect for authority and spawn some self-discipline, but he would only be punished with having to attend a First Time Offender Program, or probation for his ill-fated misdeed.

The complainant heard knocking on his rear door. He opened it several inches for the two unknown suspects and asked what they needed. The lead male pushed open the door, forcing the resident backwards, and both entered uninvited. The smaller man was holding a 12 oz. can of Bud Light beer. The larger male shoved the complainant on the chest and then upon seeing a blue bicycle at the rear door, told him "This bike is mine!" The complainant could only watch as they brought his bike down the stairs and then down an alley inside the complex, but he did see the smaller suspect drop his beer can on the ground. I arrived and contacted the complainant, broadcasting the description of the two burglars who went walking down the alley. I saw five intoxicated males that were just two buildings away and drinking the same beer brand. One of the drunken males carelessly faced my direction and urinated as I approached. I saw a blue bicycle leaning against a brick wall, and the complainant was able to retain his stolen property. He did not however see either of the two males that had been in his apartment among the five drunken males. Moments later, the larger suspect appeared from around some high bushes and started walking down the alley. The complainant pointed at him and quickly indicated that he was the first man that forced his way inside and stole his bicycle. I arrested him for burglary, called the Evidence Unit to attempt to get prints from the discarded beer can from the escaped suspect, and summoned our Paddy Wagon to transport the five intoxicated males to Detox. Maybe that would stifle their desire to be drunk at noon.

A man had been driving his cousins' vehicle for a month. During the morning hours, someone stole it. Because of its uniqueness, I just had to send out a citywide message knowing that it would certainly be spotted by a patrol officer somewhere. Two hours later an officer working the south side found the abandoned stolen vehicle, a low-rider, bright pink '87 Chevy Blazer with tinted windows, chrome rims, sunroof, "Ain't Nothin Nice" inscribed across the tailgate, a wizard as a hood ornament, and Oklahoma tags. Truly one of a kind.

For many years a man hadn't heard from a decades-long friend, but then he did. The friend called him from Iowa and would need a place to stay just short term when he got released from prison. The man picked up the ex-con at the Greyhound bus station and brought him home to live with him and his 75-year-old mother. After just a few days, the man was confronted with the reality that he was now living with an ex-con that abused drugs and alcohol, and being a dutiful friend paid for him to go to rehab.

After only 5 days, he was approved to be released briefly for Thanksgiving, but then brought home a friend who was also downcast. The homeowner went to sleep about 1:30 a.m., leaving his two guests in his home drinking beer in his kitchen. When he and his mother awakened later that morning, he discovered that his guests were unappreciative of his support, and prison had not reformed them. All his weapons that had been neatly displayed in a corner had been stolen by them. He knew they had left in a Wisconsin registered vehicle but didn't have the tag number. His long-time friend had been so fixated on stealing the guns that he left behind the envelope stuffed with his own personal papers. The two crack cocaine addicts hauled off two shotguns, two scoped rifles, two .22 caliber rifles, a 9mm pistol, and a .38 revolver. They had been given a chance to redeem themselves in the care of an immensely generous friend. They had a good chance to in time successfully reintegrate into society but had been foolhardy and chose to return to the thug life.

I stopped a young man for a traffic violation who had a most unusual name of "Mad Max" as his legal first name on his driver license. I was amused, so I asked which one of his parents was the Mel Gibson fan from the movie "Road Warriors". He was confused and didn't know what I was talking about.

A cab driver ran a red light, and I stopped him for the violation. He looked at me for 10 seconds before he finally lowered his window to speak to me. He had a wretched sorrowful look upon his face, but I didn't detect any alcohol or drugs. I concluded that he was just tired and exhausted. I took his DL back to my cruiser and returned with a ticket at most three minutes later. His head was tilted back on the headrest, and he was already snoring. I woke him up to sign the citation and told him that he needed to turn onto the next side street because he needed to get some sleep. He told me that his dad had died recently, and he hadn't been sleeping well. I watched him drive away and pass numerous streets, not heeding my safety advice. I phoned his dispatcher and framed the encounter. He knew about the driver's emotional distress and strain and said that he would have him return to the office and tell him to take the day off to thwart a potential wreck and catastrophe and lawsuit.

Two teenaged friends were carrying around a large plastic storage box loaded with candy bars that they were selling to earn money in a scholarship program. Three other teenaged boys walked past one of them, but then turned to jump and pummel the other boy a half dozen times, forcing him to collapse to the ground, then ran off having stolen his $128 of Candy. The suspects hadn't realized that they had accosted this kid on the front yard of a boy that knew them. He had witnessed the crime and attended the same school and spoke with the victims afterwards to tell them the suspects' first names. A day later I went to that middle school and had the boy witness plucked from class. He remembered their last names too, though they were a year older than him and were now in High School. I obtained their DOB's and addresses from the Attendance Coordinator, and supplemented my robbery report from the day before, thereby solving the case for the detective.

A man suffering from paranoia was jumping on cars at an Exxon station, pleading with people to help him by giving him a ride because people with guns were chasing him. I spotted the disturbed man nearby and as I approached him he flagged me down to get my attention. He ran over to ask me to stop the men with guns that were chasing him. I told him that he was safe, that no one was after him. I suspected that he had mental issues even before contact because of his alleged actions at the Exxon, and prior to that the comments said that he had tossed a wheelchair and had broken a car window. I handcuffed him and he admitted to having smoked crack cocaine in the previous two hours. I told him to get into the squad car, but he refused by saying that we were going to have to shoot him because he wasn't going. A couple more requests did nothing, so we tried without much success to push on him while trying to bend his long legs. Finally, when I threatened to mace him in the face, he yielded. We drove him to the owner of the car with the smashed front window and he was positively identified as the perpetrator. He couldn't be arrested for misdemeanor criminal mischief because we didn't witness it, so I just made the offense report, and we took him to Detox for being high. He stated that he had trouble differentiating between delusions and reality.

After swapping handcuffs, I had to wash off his blood and thin strands of his skin inside my cuffs that had peeled off during his struggle with us to resist transportation.

An ex-boyfriend drove to Dallas from an adjacent state. He parked in the parking lot where his ex-girlfriend lived, used a knife to cut his own wrists and throat, and went to knock on his ex's door. She answered and opened the door to a horrifically bloody scene, and desperately tried to stem the blood flowing from his throat. She had called 911 screaming and crying, and the call was originally dispatched as a domestic. It was bumped up to a Code 3 call for a "cutting". The Field Training Officer arrived with his rookie and began to rush over on foot to the ghastly scene. Realizing that the police had arrived, and that the ambulance was coming, the man concluded that his suicide may not be successful, so he switched to plan B. He stood up with an extended arm, the knife in his hand held at head level and pointed at the oncoming officers, then ran toward them. The Training Officer yelled to his rookie "Shoot!" The rookie's training kicked in, and he drew his pistol and fired one shot through the man's heart, killing him instantly. Suicide by cop. I had just started my shift and was sent to the location Code 3. I only completed putting up some crime scene tape and made sure that no one entered the crime scene. There was a heavy blood trail from the car of the deceased to the apartment door.

A man saw his girlfriend drive into a shopping center parking lot. He walked over to her vehicle and they began to argue. A minute later he pulled her from the car and started to slap her. She ran inside a tanning salon and told a staff member to phone 911, which he did. The suspect entered the business, pulled her over a counter and tussled with her as he dragged her back outside and then threw her onto the hood of her car. The male employee who had called 911 rushed out to her aid and pulled the suspect off the woman. We arrived to find a security guard visibly shaken, upset and crying. Turned out that he was in uniform, in front of his security office. He was being paid to prevent situations like these, but he was the suspect and the cause of it all. He went to jail for domestic violence.

In the summer of 1991, I was attending physical therapy routinely to strengthen my broken right leg (See "Dallas Cop" Volume 1). I would start with a whirlpool for circulation, do some stretching exercises, and then commence to give my leg a workout.

During one session I met a guy with long red hair and a mustache. I thought that this hippie probably did drugs. Didn't they all? I knew that I was unfairly stereotyping this quiet patient. He didn't say much; I did most of the talking. As a proud young rookie officer with Dallas PD, it didn't take long for me to mention my occupation. He was more guarded about his life. I remember being judgmental, feeling good about my station in life, and taking pity on him, though I knew nothing about him.

I saw this thirtyish man the next time that I had a Physical Therapy session. I liked talking with him, it was unforced and effortless. When he felt comfortable enough with me, he left me dumbstruck with his admission; he too was a Dallas police officer. Not wanting to blow his cover with me until he verified my identity, he was understandably cautious before he told me of his being an undercover Narcotics Officer. While in his personal vehicle, he had been rear-ended by a Domino's Pizza Delivery driver during a time when if your pizza was not delivered to you within thirty minutes, it was free. He was tossed forward from the crash and his knees struck the dashboard. He had been told that he probably wouldn't be running any long distances for the rest of his life. For most people, that wouldn't be much of a disappointment, but it seriously cramped his lifestyle because he was a long-distance runner by hobby for the joy and peace of it. We spoke several more times on subsequent visits, and then I never saw him again. I recalled the dedication that he had for his job and the burning desire he had to return to Narcotics asap. I was sure that he was there. He was. Less than six months later, he was involved in an undercover drug buy operation in a car at night, two officers with two suspects. Other officers in the shadows had them under surveillance and knew the seating arrangements in the car. The occupants of the car stepped out briefly, then went back inside. The covert officers watching wrongly assumed that the officers had not changed their seating positions, a misfortune that would have dire consequences. Soon these officers observing from the perimeter saw muzzle flashes and heard gun fire erupt inside the vehicle. Those officers quickly but cautiously scrambled toward the vehicle, firing their weapons at the suspects as they did. The two suspects inside were killed, but so was my new friend. By all accounts he was the quintessential Narcotics officer and a fine man. Tragically and regrettably, it was later determined by ballistics that he was a casualty of friendly fire.

An 11-year-old boy was sick and stayed home from school. At 9:30 a.m. he heard some tapping noises on a window. By the time he checked that window, there was nothing there, but he did see a suspect carrying a crowbar walking around in the fenced backyard, having apparently climbed over the locked chain link fence gate. The scared nervous boy called his father at work, who called the police. I arrived first and ran with a drawn pistol to the backyard, but no suspect. The boy had seen me from inside and stepped outside, and I received and broadcasted a good description of the suspect. I searched the neighborhood and spied the suspect as he was standing on his tippy toes about ten feet away from another home's picture window straining to peer inside. As I approached the suspect he began to walk away. I intercepted and questioned him. He playacted unconvincingly, telling me that he was looking for a friend. Interrogating him further, he gave a street name where his friend lived but we weren't on it. He couldn't call him because despite this being a middle-class neighborhood, his friend didn't have a phone. I saved him further embarrassment and ended his charade, taking him over to the boy who fingered him as the intruder. He was arrested for a ticket warrant and Criminal Trespassing.

It was a rare day on February 2, 1996. An inch of snow had blanketed the city. For the only time in my career, I drove to the service area and had them put chains on my rear tires, as all roads were unplowed.

I received a call regarding a car that had possibly been stolen. I checked the tag on my computer, and it was stolen two days earlier. A woman poked her head out into the cold from her front door across the street and said that it had just arrived night before last. She saw two teenaged boys in the car, one of whom she knew. Not thinking that they were possibly the thieves, she warned them that the car might be stolen and that they were getting their fingerprints all over it. The boys suddenly became nervous and alarmed and left. I listed the known boy as a suspect. One of the boys had printed a message in the snow on the vehicle rear window "I did it in here (Sex)".

A man entered a large electronic store well known by police for their active Loss Prevention team. The team monitored him on their security camera system and watched him as he removed two headsets from their blister packages and placed them in his left front pants pocket. He tried to walk out with the $70 products but was stopped at the exit. We arrived to arrest him, and he told us that he was exacting some vengeance upon the store for making him feel humiliated when they questioned one of his previous returns, as well as saying that he needed to go to church later. My partner and I smiled, and I remarked "Thou Shalt not Steal, wasn't that one of the Ten Commandments?" He replied "Hey, no one's perfect". On the road to jail he commented that he was a real ass for trying to get back at them, and that he was so stupid. We agreed because he had $549 cash in his wallet.

I saw four men fishing from a pier at White Rock Lake, and three of them had beer that they tried to shield from my view. I wrote one drunk male a ticket for Alcohol in the Park, then released him to a sober friend to drive him home rather than hauling him to Detox. Another male on the dock could've told me in the beginning that his name and DOB would bring up a felon with a deportation warrant from ICE, since he had it happen before when another officer questioned him about it, but he just let me sort it out. He was, however, a "10-X", or a known dangerous offender who had been arrested before for Injury to an Elderly Person, and …Murder. He said many years ago he had killed a rival gang member when he was in a gang.

The only violation that he had was also Alcohol in a Park, so I cited him. He left since his friends were now gone. The passage of enough time calms the violent beast in most all criminals.

I was working a task force one night around 11 p.m. and had a woman on a traffic stop for having busted through a stop sign. As I was talking to her, I saw two young males walking on the other side of the street. They noticed me too because of course my emergency lights were flashing. One of them was drinking from a bottle. I shifted my attention back to the motorist and then heard the "Klinkety-Klink" sound of a glass bottle striking objects. I glanced back up at the males again, and it was obvious that the one who had been carrying the bottle was now empty handed, having tossed his bottle into a narrow patch of woods. I wasn't certain as to which of them had the bottle, so I pointed at them and sternly said "YOU! COME HERE!" The guilty party separated from his friend and came to me. He received a ticket for littering and went to jail for 9 ticket warrants.

Many times, when I noticed an ambulance on emergency approaching me from my rear, I would activate my emergency lights and siren and race ahead to block the next major intersection to enable the ambulance to improve their response time in a life-threatening situation. I would do this carefully and when the ambulance cleared the intersections, I would race ahead and continue doing it until they turned onto a different street. I'm sure the paramedics appreciated it, and I had fun in the process. Despite improving the fire engine or ambulance response time, I could have been reprimanded. They were authorized to drive Code 3, but I was not.

Years ago, Dallas was having problems with burglars ramming the rear of their vehicle through the front door/window of a closed pharmacy or convenient store, then quickly loading up the safe or ATM onto the bed or trunk. They were experienced and proficient and didn't worry about breaking into the safe or ATM for the cash until they were safely at home in a garage. If caught, they rarely cooperated and often stated they would do their time in prison and when released, do it all over again.

The Department distributed pictures and names of the known safe burglars. I was surprised that there were 100 males, and 5 females, ALL the same race.

On a related call that I once took, there were 5 empty safes and ATM's that I had pulled from a shallow creek in a park over a short stretch of about 100 yards. They were extracted and loaded onto a city contract wrecker via their cable and sent to the auto pound because of their size.

While waiting for a signal light to change, my rookie and I noticed a woman crying in her car next to us. She was wailing loudly and occasionally hit her steering wheel. I lowered my window and waved my arm to get her attention. "Ma'am is everything okay? Can we help you?" Still sobbing, she yelled mournfully "He cheated on me!!" In a subdued tone, I said "We're sorry." As we drove off, I told my rookie that we could help her with a beater, but not with a cheater.

Several males were drinking in a front yard. I arrived to find six males standing around a pickup truck on the street drinking 12 oz. bottles of Bud Light. Three received public intoxication citations and were released to the three others who were cited for consuming alcohol on a public street. They took our advice and brought their beer into the house and backyard. It was 10:30 a.m. on a Sunday morning.

A suspect came by the complainant's apartment at 6 a.m. and started knocking on her door. She looked through the side window to get a visual of her unexpected visitor and the suspect pointed a chrome handgun at her and pulled the trigger. She heard the click of the pistol hammer. The woman told the suspect to go home to his wife, though he'd been her boyfriend for 12 years. He replied that he wasn't leaving until she opened the door which he started to pound with his fist. She didn't want to involve her neighbors, so she let him inside, only to be shoved to the floor and have him kick her foot. The suspect stood over her, aimed at her head, and once again pulled the trigger. She heard another hammer click. The suspect insisted that she needed to make up her mind whether she wanted him in her life. She said not since she found out about another mistress, and she was going to call his wife and tell her everything just as soon as she arrived at work. The suspect soon left the apartment. She did use three-way calling from work and spoke to the suspect who was unaware that his cousin was covertly listening, but after the call the cousin preferred to be uninvolved. The woman was also worried because the suspect had promised to retaliate and inform her separated husband and children if she exposed their relationship to his wife. Those who live in glass houses shouldn't throw stones.

A woman was happy because she had placed her cheap, worn shoes under a shoe rack at the back of the store and was now walking toward the exit, soon to be the proud owner of an expensive but stolen pair of shoes on her feet. Her glee was interrupted by a beeper on the Sensor-Matic that detected the sensor in her shoes because it hadn't been deactivated by a cashier upon purchase. She was arrested after we arrived.

I received a call involving a man driving with two flat tires on the right side, often an indication of bouncing off the street curbs from drunkenness. I found the vehicle stopped with the man stooped over one of the flat tires in his failed attempts to change it. Both deflated tires were off the rims. His movements were so unsteady and comically slow, it was obvious that he was inebriated. I announced "Police" and told him to stand up. This quickly disturbed what little equilibrium he had, and he toppled over backwards onto the ground. After I helped him to his feet, he failed all my sobriety tests. Two witnesses had observed him driving. So, the drunken 30-year-old was taken to jail at 11:30 a.m. for what turned out to be his third DWI arrest, a felony. He had a 750 ml bottle of 80 Proof Vodka in his car that was ¾ empty.

It was dark one Fall evening at 7:45 p.m. when I rode my bicycle up to a lone vehicle facing the lake in an otherwise empty parking lot. I saw no one nearby and postulated that there might be a couple inside exploring their sexuality. When I was alongside the driver's side rear door, I lifted and tilted my handlebar so that my light shined into the back seat. Though the window was tinted, I could discern that a woman was leaning her back against the door for support. Her legs were spread wide open, and a man's head was halfway under her skirt. I quickly opened the door and the woman had to brace herself to keep from falling backwards. The man however was still oblivious to my new presence, not having heard the door open nor noticed that the dome light had illuminated the interior. The woman had turned her head to see me, but soon realized that the man was aloof to the present circumstances, so she lightly slapped his head to get his attention. The man looked up and with widened eyes exclaimed "We're clothed! We're clothed! We have our clothes on!" I informed him that I could see that but that they were still doing something that they shouldn't be doing, and I needed their ID. They stepped out of the car and the man gave me his DL. The woman said that she didn't have her ID and gave me her info verbally. She was embarrassed and cold, so I let her sit in the car while I wrote the man a ticket for "Obscene Conduct", a form of Disorderly Conduct. When I began to write, it was obvious that my disruption had caused him to lose some composure. He shook his head and smiled. I told him how unlucky he was, that I was the only officer at this 9.3-mile radius lake at this time and that I just happened to be here at that moment. Still smiling, the man confided to me that he had just started two or three minutes before my interruption. My use of a patrol officer's computer determined that the woman had lied to me about her name. Further processing showed that she had a CA DL and she confessed to being that person. She had no warrants, and I could see by the expression on the man's face that he was disappointed that his newly acquainted co-worker had given me needless drama and lied to a police officer. She was cited for Obscene Conduct and Fail to ID.

I went to Parkland Hospital for several hours to watch a felony prisoner. His arresting officer told me the story that this arrestee was drunk, and rear ended another vehicle. He stepped out to run from the scene trying not to let his below-the-knee prosthetic right leg slow him down. The man whose vehicle he had struck thought his attempt to flee was absurd and soon caught up to him. The arrestee though wasn't going to cooperate and turned trying to stab his pursuer, who backed off and let the drunk limp away. The police found him, and he hobbled away into a narrow-wooded area that was a sloped embankment to a creek a dozen foot below. When the drunk slipped and fell, his duct-taped limb detached. Two officers nabbed him and took him into custody. He had crack cocaine in his pockets and even a stash in his false limb. Later, during our guard duty of him he began to sober up and motioned to me with his forefinger to come over and talk to him. Hoping to nullify the implicating drug evidence found on his person, he insisted "The drugs not mine! The drugs not mine!"

Two 19-year-olds robbed a 72-year-old woman of her purse, and she fell to the ground when one suspect pushed her. An alert witness remembered the license plate of the vehicle as the suspects sped away. We correctly assumed that the registered address was probably incorrect, so we had the dispatcher search the ticket file for any recent and more local addresses. We were lucky. We had an officer go to check for the vehicle in the complex parking lot, and he found it. After several officers waited inconspicuously around the perimeter for an undercover Deployment officer to tell us when the vehicle became occupied, we got impatient from waiting and went to the apartment. A woman had ticket warrants linked to that address, and a woman came to the door and allowed us to enter. Though it was 3 p.m., she said she had been tired from looking for work and we had just aroused her from her slumber. There in plain view sprawled out on the coffee table were several credit cards. I looked at them and they all belonged to our elderly complainant, as did the wallet on the coffee table and the purse beneath it. Another nearby purse was checked as the woman tried to dissuade our enthusiasm by telling us that it was hers. She lied. There was just a Sam's Club card belonging to some man in it, nothing else. Now her explanation changed to her having just found it in the parking lot and she didn't know what to do with it. She was dumbfounded and speechless when I told her if that was true, she could've just called the police. A credit card belonging to yet another man was found in plain sight lying atop the kitchen counter. The woman told us that the two men that had been in the apartment had gone to the store. We still had five squad cars parked at various locations around the apartment complex. Two other officers on the call waited in the apartment with the woman. We kept the evidence in our squad car and converged with other officers in an isolated corner of the complex that had no outer drives, waiting to get word from an undercover officer that the suspects had returned so we could pounce. Suddenly, the officer announced that one of the suspects was heading up the stairs (we had the clothing description from our victim). We drove our cars toward the apartment but by the time we arrived the suspect had already been grabbed and handcuffed by the officers waiting inside the apartment. The suspect vehicle was searched, and a shotgun was found as well as a realistic looking BB gun pistol. Inside a leather jacket front pocket from the car was a wallet from another man who had been robbed three days before. That man had been robbed at the same time as the man whose credit card was found on the kitchen counter. Both the woman and the one suspect in our custody needed to be interrogated, so they were both brought to speak with Robbery detectives and later went to jail. Other charges like Robbery, Aggravated Robbery, Burglary of a Motor Vehicle, Theft, and Credit Card Abuse were sure to follow from related cases. The recovered property eventually was all returned to the true owners.

Riding bicycles, we caught up to a motorist that was on the street and wasn't wearing his seatbelt when he stopped in his apartment complex. After making contact, he immediately had an attitude and began to raise his voice. Besides getting the attention of some neighbors his anger also stirred his brother who was quick to come over and intervene to show support. He had a worse attitude problem, and we told him a few times to chill because his brother was only receiving a ticket. He didn't abate or retreat despite being told to back off and that his continued interference would result in his arrest for interfering with our official duties. There was no convincing him to cooperate, he just had to be Mr. Tough Guy and be protective of his brother. We arrested him, and a short time later in the back seat of the police cruiser he calmed down and admitted the stupidity of his pigheaded altercation.

A woman's boyfriend from 4 years before came to her front door while she was inside at the rear of her apartment. He was looking for her brother, but she told her friend not to let him inside because it might cause problems with her absent husband, and she didn't trust him, believing him to be a thief. Her friend let him inside anyway. The woman rushed to the front of her apartment and started pushing on her Ex, angrily ordering him to get out. The reaction upset him, and he pulled out a black 9mm pistol from inside the front of his pants, then pointed it at her saying "I'll shoot you bitch!" He left the apartment and entered the passenger side of a primer gray vehicle. I arrived and she informed me of his description and that he might be at a convenience store at the front of the complex. I relayed that info to my cover officer who found the vehicle at that location. I drove there and we took the suspect into custody. When I searched the passenger side of the vehicle, I discovered his pistol beneath the seat. It had been stolen. He went to jail for Aggravated Assault and several ticket warrants.

A week later I had another call to the same location. The same woman had allowed another woman to stay for a few days, but now wanted her out. As she was gathering her things, the man that I had arrested showed up to assist with her move. He recognized me and was polite and smiling. The woman had dropped the charges against him, meaning that I had wasted my time. "I told you she's crazy" said the smiling man who just a week before had pointed a gun at her and threatened to shoot her.

A few apartment complexes on a short street were having issues with the same several males dealing drugs. Some arrests had been made, but the dopers continued to ply their trade. On a chilly Sunday afternoon, one of those males--a 29-year-old--was standing inside of a wrought iron fence watching the street for customers. A call came out regarding a man being down by the sidewalk, possibly drunk. On my way there, the call was reported though this time a comment was added that it was a possible shooting, so I stepped it up to Code 3 driving and passed the ambulance that was enroute to the call. I arrived and was the first person at the motionless man's side. Several neighbors from apartments were visible and told me that he might be shot because they heard a gunshot before seeing him on his left side. I moved his arm to look at his face and shook him to be sure he wasn't just drunk. Fluid oozed from his mouth onto the ground. He wasn't drunk, he was dead, having been shot in the back of his head. I alerted the dispatcher of his demise and started the needed units. No one saw a shooter, they only heard the method of death, and knew that he was a regular who slung dope. It was a perilous way to make a living, and there was a good likelihood that a competitor could increase his sales and make more money by having him eliminated.

A suspect went to a cashier to use a $100 Traveler's Check to pay for a $35 bottle of perfume. The cashier was unsure how to process the check and called over her supervisor who knew of previous incidents of counterfeit Traveler Checks being presented. She compared the check to a colored brochure that she had and phoned an 800 number. The check number was confirmed as counterfeit. The suspect was detained and waited for us to arrive. When we did, I spoke to the same person at the 800 number but was told that the check owner's personal information for verification and report purposes had to come from the Security Division in New York. We couldn't reach them, so we could only make an offense report and not an arrest report, meaning that the suspect could not be arrested at this time. The suspect had no ID, so she was taken to be fingerprinted and then released. Two other unused Traveler checks were found between her pants and under her waistband, and these were put in the property room. She would escape justice, but only temporarily. Once a Detective contacted the Security Division to confirm that the check was counterfeit, a warrant would be issued for her arrest.

A couple had been living together for several months. The woman had gone out the night before without this common law husband. He wrongly suspected that she might be talking to a man when he caught her on the phone, but it was only one of her female friends. He started to make false accusations against her and shoved her onto the bed. While still shouting at her, she slipped past him and ran out of the bedroom into the hallway. There he caught up with her and choked her with both hands making it difficult for her to breathe. She made it to the kitchen where she exhibited a knife and told him to get out. He stepped out the door for only a few seconds but then returned. By now the woman was wielding a .38 special handgun. Given his history of domestic abuse she feared for her safety and sternly ordered him to get out. The suspect maneuvered and overpowered the complainant by putting her in a headlock and took the pistol away from her and put it in his car. Still angry, he returned but was again confronted by the complainant holding a knife for protection. This was the scene that I walked into when I arrived. I arrested the suspect, and the woman collapsed to the floor crying and visibly shaken from her terrifying ordeal.

Two men entered a grocery store together. One of them was recognized as a shopper who just a week before was seen with a handful of lip and eyeliner pencils in his hand. When an employee asked him at that time if he wanted to pay for them, he embarrassingly put them back on the shelf and swiftly exited the store. Here he was in the store again, and with another male. They were watched. Sure enough, they returned to the cosmetic section and hurriedly and covertly (or so they thought) rolled up eye liner and lip liner pens into a bundle inside their T-shirts and waistbands. They were halted as they tried to leave and taken to the office. We arrived and returned 165 eye and lip liner pens valued at $1,000.00 and confiscated an additional $300.00 of the same property from the back seat of their vehicle. Both thieves had prior theft convictions and were therefore charged with an enhanced Felony Theft.

A woman had a knock at her door at 3:30 a.m. She was surprised but happy to see a 45-year-old male friend that she hadn't seen in nearly a year. He had driven there drunk after he had a dispute with his girlfriend. The female friend invited him inside. She was used to seeing him intoxicated; he was drunk when they met 10 years earlier, and she had always known him as an alcoholic. They conversed for almost two hours to get caught up on each other's lives and then the man used the bathroom. While he was in there, she heard a "thud" and entered the bathroom to see if he was okay because he wasn't responding to her concerned calls from outside the door. She found him lying on the floor, either passed out or knocked out. He had a one-inch gash above his right eyebrow. She slapped him in the face for him to regain his consciousness, and then held an ice pack on his laceration to minimize the swelling. After he sobered up a bit from some coffee, she allowed him into her bed to sleep as they were now both very tired. She told him that he had a little yellow tinge. He chuckled and joked that he didn't have much of a liver left. When she awakened in the mid-morning, she was next to a dead man. Had he died from the accumulated liver damage from decades of heavy alcohol consumption, or was his death from a mortal wound to his head from his fall? The Medical Examiner's Office retrieved him for an examination to be certain.

A sad woman in her 50's called a Social Services worker and during their conversation said that when her medication arrived, she was just going to overdose and end it all. The concerned social worker phoned police to report a potential suicide. I took the call and rapped on the door when I arrived at the apartment. The woman answered and was very surprised to see me. She inquired as to who had called me and why I was there. We don't typically reveal the identity of the reporting person, but since the caller was just a nameless voice over the phone, I told her. A moment later I walked over to a small living room table to confiscate a revolver, opened the spindle, and removed six bullets and placed them on the other side of the room by the fireplace. Asked why she had a loaded pistol so accessible, she admitted that she was upset and that she did tell the social worker that she was going to commit suicide. She calmly added that it was an empty threat because she didn't have the courage to actually do it. She explained that her son had joined a cult, and that cult members occasionally came by her apartment. Her son had already stolen $20,000.00 from their safety deposit box, including a rare coin collection, and removed all her furniture from a storage unit. She felt helpless to stop him, and very alone. He had disowned his mother by telling her that she was no longer his mother and that he didn't need her anymore. He was part of a much larger family now. I gave her the phone number of an officer who was a cult expert and released her into the care and custody of a good friend for her safety.

A drenching downpour had unloaded so much water in so little time that when it stopped a narrow creek had risen to flood over about 100 yards of roadway. It was obvious to me that an attempt to cross would be foolish and futile, so I positioned my police cruiser as a blockade to prevent passage by any impatient and recklessly ambitious driver. But I could only stop vehicles from my side of the swollen creek. It was only a matter of time before a fool hardy driver from the other side didn't just get their tires wet and U-turn but attempted a crossing. Several pickup trucks had determined that the road was impassable and that it wasn't worth the risk, but two women in a car disregarded common sense and decided to gamble and drive slowly thru the water. They stalled out as I watched from my squad car on the other side. They waited in their car for a few minutes fully expecting me to wade out to their car and escort them twenty yards to higher ground. I stepped to the water's edge and told them that they needed to abandon their car in case the water was still rising. They reluctantly did so, and as they walked thru the foot of water toward me a newspaper photographer snapped a picture from the far side. The picture appeared in the next days' Dallas Morning News. I received some good-natured ribbing for my lack of chivalry and my misspelled name in the paper, but should I be wet for the rest of the day because they ignored many higher chassis vehicles that had turned around? I assessed that the twenty yards was safe to walk across, and I would've sprung into action if one had lost her footing.

In mid evening my rookie and I responded to a cutting call and soon were searching for the suspect. Three of us went to the front door of the apartment on our call sheet to look for this suspect when a woman (later determined to be her sister) shouted to us from the parking lot "That's my apartment." She must've seen her sister in the apartment pass by a lit window because she also told us the person that we were looking for was coming to the front door from inside the apartment. We contacted her and quickly determined that she was our assault suspect and began to make the arrest. At this same moment the sister from the parking lot was now at the apartment and she was told by my rookie that she needed to wait for us to finish arresting her sister before she could enter. Having no patience and no sense she sharply retorted "Motherfucker you can't keep me out of my apartment!" and uttered more profanities. Continuing to denigrate us, her loud antics began to attract a large crowd of people who were already outside, and their presence became a safety issue. My rookie continued to stand in front of us and in front of the belligerent woman so that we could complete the arrest of her sister who was also being uncooperative. There was no room for the anxious sister to enter the apartment without jeopardizing our safety as we were making the arrest at the doorway. She pointed her finger at the rookie's forehead and told him to let her into the apartment, still using profanity and said, "That's my sister!" and attempted to step around the young officer. The officer sidestepped to block her path and then thankfully noticed that she pulled something from her left side, a thirteen-inch butcher knife with a seven-inch blade that was now pointed skyward with the blade facing him and getting closer. He reacted quickly and shoved her to the ground, and she dropped her knife. He prevented injury to himself and perhaps to us by this action and alerted us by saying she had a knife. He quickly moved to handcuff her, overcoming her resistance. She was charged with Interference with the Official Duties of a Public Servant and Aggravated Assault on a Public Servant. The two sisters remained angry and defiant as they sat next to each other in the back seat on the way to jail, yelling and cursing us the entire way.

Two women had been involved in a relationship and lived together for 22 years. They had been arguing and edgy for several days over financial concerns. They had no food, no electricity, no phone, and no money. During one of the verbal alterations one of them grabbed her black purse and swung it against the back of her lover's head, causing a laceration. The victim went across the street to a neighbor's house and told him of their quarrel and he phoned police. We arrived to find our complainant with a bloodied front and rear shirt collar and bloody matted hair, then went back to arrest our 63-year-old suspect for Family Violence Assault.

A man's neighbor walked over to his house and told him that he had just witnessed a male wearing a red cap and white T shirt steal his weed eater from his pickup truck. The owner quickly headed off in the direction of the suspect's travel. He found him blocks away still carrying his weed eater and told him "I got you now! I'm calling the police! You're going to jail!" The surprised suspect dropped the weed eater and ran. The owner recovered his stolen weed eater and called the police. I took the report, then searched for the suspect to no avail. I alerted an undercover officer in the area, then went on to my next call. A bit later the clandestine officer surveilled a man fitting the suspect description walk into a thrift store. By the time that I arrived another uniformed officer had taken him into custody when he stepped back out into the parking lot. My complainant--the weed eater owner--identified this male as the same suspect that he had seen with his weed eater earlier and he was taken to be interviewed by a detective. There, the suspect could not provide a written confession statement because he was illiterate but did confess to having stolen the weed eater from the truck. He provided his "mark" for the detective. He had said that he wanted to sell it to get some money so that he could buy some clothes for a later job interview (he was found in a thrift store).

On a call, I arrived at the community center of a low-income government subsidized apartment building and had a janitor tell me "He went that way officer. He's going down the hall trying to get back to his room." He told me the name of the suspect and added that he was in a wheelchair. We looked down the hallway and we could see the suspect in the distance frantically rolling his wheelchair to his door. I dashed down the hallway and just before I reached his door, he was able to slip inside and deadbolt it. The doors were well-built, sturdy steel doors and unless the occupant slid open the deadbolt from the inside there was no easy way of gaining access even with a key. I tried to get him to open the door, but he was aware of that outcome. He cursed at us from the inside in a very high-pitched voice saying, "Ah ain't crazy! You ain't comin in here to get me you Motherfuckers! Why you cops always hassling me? Get outta here you shit headed Motherfuckin' pigs!" etcetera.

The janitor had been mopping the community room floor and was about to enter a hallway to mop when the paraplegic blocked his way and stated that he wasn't coming in there. The wheelchair suspect then pulled out a 4-inch bladed knife and wheeled himself towards the janitor, holding his knife with an out stretched arm like it was a lance. The janitor spun his mop around and poked the suspect on the chest with the handle, effectively keeping him away.

I just filed Aggravated Assault at large on the suspect, as there was no rush and no way to bypass the heavy metal door and frame. We knew who he was and where he lived. He would be arrested in short order.

Two officers couldn't determine what a man sitting in a pickup truck was doing when they saw him in the dark facing White Rock Lake. They were curious and stepped out and shined their flashlights on him. He was holding a box cutter to his throat. The officers stepped away and called for a supervisor, other officers, an ambulance, and some crime scene tape to keep lake goers away. This last request led me to believe that the man had already committed suicide and was dead. I arrived with my partner and brought some crime scene tape for the perimeter. A group of officers were standing around seemingly just talking but were strategizing. I shone my flashlight on the driver expecting to see a dead man, but he was still touching the box cutter to his throat. Doors locked, windows rolled up, there wasn't much we could do, our options were limited. A plan was devised and would be implemented after the ambulance arrived. One officer would tap on the passenger side window to shift his attention if only for a second, then another officer would smash the driver window with his asp, while a third officer would lean in and "dry stun" him with her taser, hopefully long enough to incapacitate him and cause him to drop his box knife. He would then be pulled from his vehicle, cuffed, and taken to a psychiatric facility. My always enthusiastic partner would deliver the dry stun. Seldom does a plan go according to plan, and this one went awry. My partner dry stunned the driver, but he failed to drop his box cutter and slightly cut his throat. Anxious and eager officers tried to help and get at the driver from behind her and bumped her enough so that she lacerated her inside arm on a shard of broken window glass that was poking up and still inside the rubber molding of the door.

She needed 14 stitches and was on light duty for several days.

A young married couple decided to avoid the wife's side of the family for the sake of their infant son. Her family was dysfunctional, with alcoholics, drug users, people on bi-polar medication, and just some unfriendly short-fused rabble rousers, as evidenced by a family fistfight that had just happened on New Year's Eve. Not being able to speak to their daughter, or see their grandson, her family had started to harass them by stalking them, calling too often, and now leaving leaflets under the wipers of cars of members of their church congregation. These flyers wrongly and deceitfully informed them that their son-in-law was troubled by alcohol and drug use and was an abusive father in need of their prayers. None of it was true, and indeed the couple was exceedingly polite and well-mannered and by all appearances quite normal. What made the leaflet plea even more disingenuous was that her father who was responsible for the leaflet distribution was an avowed atheist.

Another officer and I had just sat down to eat pizza at a popular restaurant buffet. I noticed a man walked inside from the exit only door as some people left. The young man was shabbily dressed and toting a newspaper and a carton of orange drink. He sat down just two tables away from us and began to read. Having bypassed the cashier, he hadn't paid for his pizza buffet. I sensed that as soon as we exited, he would be helping himself to some free pizza. No one had noticed him, or so he thought. I went to the pizza counter and quietly alerted the manager to his presence, telling her to keep an eye on him because he avoided having to pay for his pizza by stealthily entering from the exit door. I told her that we would return in a few minutes, and I predicted that he would be consuming unbought pizza. Sure enough, when we returned the manager was standing near his table and gave us a nod. I pulled away his plate of pizza and told him to stand up. I patted him down and found his wallet and had him step outside with us away from the crowded restaurant. He lied and told us that his phantom no show friend was going to pay for his meal. His $2.99 theft earned him a $280 theft citation. I wondered how many times he had stolen pizza that way before.

An older woman had emigrated from war-torn Bosnia. Having fled such a hostile dangerous environment, she was now living peacefully. However, it didn't take much to trigger her post traumatic stress. She returned to the apartment complex laundry room and found an 11-year-old boy on rollerblades stuffing some of her undergarments into his pants pockets. The woman screamed for police (in her own language) as she ran after the thief and recovered her clothes from his pockets. Someone called the police for this woman, and she cried nonstop during my entire visit while the complex manager/witness told me where the boy lived. As I was walking to his door, the boy rolled past me and went through his door just before me. I saw his mother and spoke to her about her adopted son's lady's underwear raids from the laundry room.

She believed me and told me that he was bi-polar and had erratic behavioral problems. I had the mother hand me the undergarments that I could see dangling out of his pant pockets, and I returned to the laundry room to locate an owner. I entered and saw another woman. She had the dryer door open and was searching through her clothes. I was holding a lady's underwear and a brassiere, and asked if they were hers. I think that she was also an immigrant that spoke no English, as she said not a word. She just stared at me strangely, and slowly and cautiously approached me to retrieve her bra and panties from what was probably the first American police officer she had ever contacted. She took her items from me, and quickly rushed out of the laundry room with her laundry basket. I think she believed that I was the thief and that by not understanding my comment, she probably thought that I was making remarks about her undergarments and trying to proposition her.

When I worked as a patrol officer, I was doggedly determined to stay busy. That meant when there were distant calls or no calls holding, I would look for a traffic stop. That had a price; not everyone was pleasant or reasonable.

I stopped a guy for speeding on my beat, driving 57 in a 35-mph zone. He immediately stepped out and went to the passenger side of his car to look for his insurance card. This never happened, so it immediately heightened my awareness. I told him to get back inside his car. He found his insurance proof, but didn't listen, and only went back to the driver side. I asked if he knew why he was being stopped, and he said no. I informed him, and he asked to see the radar. I said no and that I wasn't required to show it to him. He had a large shoulder held T.V. camera lying on his backseat, and I sensed correctly that he would try to agitate me looking for a story. "I suppose you're going to write me a ticket now!" "That is why you were stopped." The angry motorist demanded to know my name as he leaned forward to read my name tag. I pronounced it for him, and just before I turned to walk back to my cruiser, I told him to have a seat in his truck. Unsurprisingly, he didn't listen. I watched from my cruiser as he walked away but stopped at the street curb to talk to someone on his cellphone. I returned with a citation, and at first, he flattered me by saying that he used to be a police officer for 3 years, but he wouldn't do my job. Then he flip-flopped and insulted me by saying that guys like me with an attitude gave cops a bad name. I pointed out that I didn't have an attitude, but if he showed me one, he would get one in return. I extended my arm to have him sign his ticket at the "X". He took his DL from my ticket book cover, then took his sweet time to file it appropriately in his wallet. After that, he snatched the ticket book from my hand and asked how much the ticket was going to cost him. I told him there was a list of fines on the back of one of his copies. He stared at the ticket 10 seconds, and I reminded him that his signature was not a plea of guilty but a promise to take care of the ticket within 21 days. He stared at the ticket 20 more seconds. I asked if he was going to sign it, or was I going to have to sign it for him? He told me he would sign it and stared at it 30 more seconds. I reminded him that if he didn't sign it, I would sign it for him. He only wanted to rattle my cage and waited 10 more seconds and still didn't sign. I took the ticket book from him, wrote "Refused to sign" on the signature block, and handed him his copies. He quickly went into his briefcase and my hand went to my pistol until I saw him pull out a legal pad. He wrote my name down this time as he leaned in to read it. I told him to spell it right and to write down my badge number too. I reiterated to take care of his ticket within 21 days and turned to walk back to my car. "Or else what?" he barked. "Or else it becomes a warrant" "And then what are you going to do, arrest me?" "If I stop you again and you have the warrant, yes." "Guys like you with your attitude give cops a bad name! Do you work at the station down the street?" "I sure do." "What's the name of your supervisor?" "He's off today" "I don't care who is at the Station! I'll contact the Mayor if I have to! How do you say your name"? "You wrote it down, just read it". "Too many cops are jerks with attitudes!" "I've got things to do, and you've got things to do. I'm not going to sit here and argue with you all day!" "You need things to do!

You should be out there fighting crime and chasing criminals. You didn't find anything on me, did you? No warrants?" "No, but I checked, I don't know you from Adam." I walked back to my car and sat down inside. He quickly trotted back to me remarking "Too many of you guys are jerks!" I could barely step out of my car before he was upon me, and he stopped on the other side of my door. He stared at my face, hoping that I would come unglued, then smiled and asked me what I was thinking. "I hope to see you in court" was my reply. He walked back to his car and then turned back to shout "JERK!" I drove past his car and saw him glaring a big grin on his face, hoping to antagonize me. I just smiled back. He followed me until he turned into the police station parking lot, disregarding the sign that read "POLICE VEHICLES ONLY". He lodged a complaint with Internal Affairs but didn't fabricate anything that I had did or said. The worst he could report was that I had "aggressively exited" my vehicle at the end of the traffic stop which I needed to do so for my safety from his fast approach.

I went to court over his speeding ticket and brought the three pages that I had written after the traffic stop to remember how he had done his best to cause me to overact and lose my cool. The prosecutor dismissed the case before even conferring with me first. I told her of his vain attempt to intimidate and aggravate me and unfolded the notes from my pocket to show her. I asked her to refile the case, and she consented. I returned weeks later for a second court date, being completely prepared once again to testify. I appraised the different prosecutor of this case when she asked me why the case had been refiled. After speaking to the motorist, she related to me that he had pled guilty on the speeding charge, adding that he just wanted to get it over.

For a few years I parked my police cruiser in a liquor store parking lot 3 or 4 nights a week about 10 minutes before they closed at 9 p.m. for robbery and theft prevention and to assure that they closed on time per state law. I was on special assignment nearby anyways, and my police cruiser presence also benefitted a beer/wine store on one side, and another liquor store across the street. My friend was the manager at the store where I parked, and after he closed and secured the store, we would talk for a bit in the parking lot. My friend told me that 5 minutes before we stepped outside, the white car facing us across the street in the other liquor store parking lot with its headlights on had been in his lot. I had noticed another police car there 20 minutes earlier parked alongside the driver of a car, but it had gone. Curious about the white car occupant(s), I drove off and passed them, but then returned from behind and ran the tag, and shined my spotlight into the vehicle from the side as I drove by slowly. The windows were tinted, and I saw nothing. I had the license plate for future reference if I needed it, and, frankly, it was quitting time. I had my suspicions about what this might be about, and they were confirmed when I pulled into the police parking lot and hesitated long enough to see the white car pull in behind me, then turn to the front area of the patrol division where upper echelon officers parked. I rushed inside from the rear and leaned against the counter to watch who came through the front door lobby. It was my Watch Commander Lieutenant. As I expected, he circled to my location. Plopping himself next to me at the counter, his shoulder touching mine, I knew he was being slyly inquisitive when he asked me how things were going. I responded, "I haven't been drinking sir", knowing that he was sniffing my exhalation for any sign of alcohol. He tried to play it off like he didn't know what I was talking about. I told him why I was a regular at the liquor store. He pretended that his being tipped off about my possibly drinking alcohol on duty wasn't why he had struck up a conversation with me. I knew better. He rarely talked to me, and never to just chit-chat. Our dialogue ended seconds later.

I stopped a tough-looking big-bellied tattooed man for speeding. As I asked him for his DL and insurance, I noticed that he had an unusual white towel over his front middle floorboard hump. It was a large green marijuana leaf picture with the words "There is only one girl that can make a man choke-Mary Jane" (marijuana). Taking the cue, I inquired if he had any marijuana in his vehicle. He looked at me contemptuously and asked what gave me the right to ask him that question. I pointed out the towel, and he said it didn't mean that he used marijuana and added that his kid was in the car. He was a DJ, and the other side of the towel was the name of his employer, a synonym for a drug house. I commented about the implication, that his son (about 12) saw this daily and probably had a different impression, that the towel tacitly condoned the use of marijuana. When I returned to his car with the speeding ticket, he wrangled with my comment no more. He was quiet and polite rather than indignant.

We responded to a cutting call and found our complainant shaking and crying on the phone. She had a bloody nose, a lacerated finger, an abraded and bruised left arm, and a bruised back. An argument had erupted over money. Her boyfriend became so furious that he punched her in the face several times with his fists and struck her with a skillet from the kitchen while she tried to fend off the blows. She grabbed a small knife to defend herself and lacerated the back of his head. He reacted quickly and took the knife from her. She crawled towards the front door while he continued to pummel and kick her, at one point shoving her head into a wall and causing a head dent impression in the plaster. Still not finished unleashing his fury, he pulled her hair braids and forced her face onto this rising knee a few times. Luckily, her friend arrived as the beating ended and whisked her away for safety. As they were leaving, the suspect warned that he was leaving too but he'd be back with a gun.

I was there long enough to complete the assault offense report, and for the crime scene unit to fully process the scene and depart. As we were exiting the parking lot, the suspect drove into the parking lot and passed us. We had his vehicle description and circled back and intercepted him as he was stepping out of his vehicle, and he was promptly arrested. No gun was found.

The security guards inside an apartment complex approached a male who was squealing his car tires with the emergency brake applied, causing him to fishtail as he did this in different areas, even driving backwards. The guards stepped out of their patrol vehicle and told the man to stop. The drunk male sped toward them, and one guard jumped out of the way. The other guard ran out to the street because he had noticed me on a bicycle covering another officer on his traffic stop. Now two police officers accompanied him back to the complex. As the other officer reached the suspect, the suspect burned rubber again and fish-tailed once more, forcing the officer to dive out of the way to avoid being struck. The suspect squealed out of the parking lot in an effort to flee, but instead drove across and stupidly tried to jump a traffic lane that was blocked off and under repairs. His car fell three feet to the sunken lane and stopped abruptly when his front end slammed into the three feet rise on the other side of the sunken lane. Though his vehicle was obviously trapped in the sunken lane and immobile, the drunk male still had his foot trounced on the accelerator when we rushed over to extract and arrest him. He was charged with two counts of Aggravated Assault with a Motor Vehicle, Evading detention, DWI, and a warrant for DWI.

It was the upper 40's on a mid-December morning, and there were few calls. An officer attempted to detain a robbery suspect, but he took evasive action and ran across blocks and down several alleys. Though I was about 10 miles away, I hurried to insert myself into the area. As I neared an intersection, I alerted the dispatcher that I saw two or three probable suspects from the robbery walking in my same direction a block away. I thought one of them dashed off between two houses. I drove up behind the remaining two and ordered them to come back to my car and put their hands on the hood. They did so, one with a bad attitude. One of the primary officers arrived and confirmed that these were two of his suspects, so they were arrested. The smallest of the two was the oldest, having turned 17 a mere five days earlier, making him an adult in Texas. He learned this to his shock and dismay on his way to the county jail, believing himself to be taken to juvenile. His cockiness and bravado disintegrated when he became aware that he was going to the adult jail. Some female arrestees at the jail were amused by him, one calling him a runt. A female jailer said aloud "Hey! What's that 4th grader doing in here?" and got some laughs. The paperwork for the two primary officers assigned to this Aggravated Robbery was extensive to process the three juveniles and one adult. It was the first time in my then 15-year career that I had one hour of overtime from having only been on one call during my entire shift.

A bar closed at 2 a.m. one Sunday morning, and a man saw that his wife had entered another man's pick-up truck, and they were about to leave. The husband rushed over to the truck, yanked the man from the truck, then beat him. After some arguing with his wife, the married couple went home. Hours later -- but still early Sunday morning -- the wife called police and told us that her husband had many warrants, including a probation violation. We checked and it was true, so we went into the house to the back bedroom where he had been presumed to be sleeping. The door was locked. Eventually, he unlocked and opened it to us. We stepped inside and told him to put some shoes on because he was going to jail for his warrants. As he was looking into his closet for a shirt, I noticed a line of whisked blood drops on the back wall, and some blood drops on his white bedsheet. I asked him where the blood came from, and he casually remarked "Oh, I just cut my wrist with a razor blade". Then he turned to face us, and we saw blood was dripping from his left wrist. We summoned an ambulance and had his wife get us a clean rag to staunch the drops of blood. I rode with the suspect in the ambulance to the hospital where he received 16 stitches. Several hours later we took him to jail.

A man accidentally elbowed a woman on the side of her head when he raised his right arm. Some words were exchanged, and the woman called the police. I arrived behind another officer and we spoke with the complainant. The older officer suggested that I go inside the store while he waited with the female complainant. I pondered why I was going inside the store to look for the suspect with a store security guard while the officer waited needlessly out of harm's way, but decided that I was better off with the younger, stronger guard to assist me if the suspect became hostile.

We found the suspect inside listening to a cassette on a demo stereo. He removed his headphones to speak with me and responded that there was no issue with the woman because he apologized, though the woman said he never did. I obtained his ID for a report, and he was warrant free on a subject check. His running commentary offered an insight into his troubled mind. He said this kind of thing happened to him all the time because he was a professional boxer and a recording artist. He had just released his first tape and they were being sold all around the world. People knew he was famous, and they were wanting to cause him problems (I wondered why they didn't want his autograph if that was true). His delusions of grandeur grew when he told me that he had been talking with the FBI about the problems he had since he cut his demo tape. I looked at the tape and there was no mention of his name; it was some kind of Zen Meditation tape. He received a criminal trespass warning and was sent on his way.

I don't drink much alcohol, so I rarely have a need to go into a liquor store. When I do, it would usually be to purchase a bottle of wine to bring to someone's house for dinner. It's not a place where I would expect to have a happenstance encounter.

I was standing in a line of about 10 people when a man several customers up from me looked back at me and stared. He said aloud "Hey man, why did you arrest me?" I tried to ignore him, but he persisted with the same question. I told him he had the wrong guy, but he wasn't buying it. "You just arrested me I know it's you! Why did you arrest me?" Knowing he wasn't going to let this go, I told him "I arrested you because were drunk in public. Are you drunk in public again?" "No sir!" A couple of customers smiled, and the man didn't say another word.

Working at Sam's Club one night, I was walking and pushing the carted money box for the girl making the occasional cash register money pulls. A middle-aged woman hurriedly walked to me and frantically told me that someone had just stole her wallet. I asked from where, and she pointed to the customer service desk. We walked over, and she told me that she had been waiting there with her daughter and turned away from the counter. When she turned back, her wallet was gone. I inquired if she had noticed anyone near her, staring at her, or if anybody had asked her questions to try and distract her. Her response was no, nobody, but that I had to stop them! "Stop who?" I replied. "The person that took my wallet! Don't you understand?" "Ma'am. I can't stop the person that stole your wallet if I don't know who it was." "Can't you make an announcement and tell them to return my wallet?" "If someone stole your wallet, they 're not going to return it" "No! The person that took my wallet is getting away!" "Ma'am, I don't have a suspect, I can't search 300 people in the store!" "Well, somebody has my wallet. It's that managers fault! I want to speak to a manager. If he hadn't told me to go to the shorter line over here, this never would've happened! He's responsible for this!" A manager walked over, and she told him the story, and again implicated the manager that directed her to a shorter line, adding that she is an attorney and will be creating a whole lot of paperwork. I interceded and asked her how it's the manager's fault because he was being courteous by having her go to a short line? She snapped "You're not being helpful; I don't think I need you!" I informed her that if she wanted to make a report, I would be over there, as I pointed.

A short time later I discovered that the over reactive alarmist had mistakenly left her wallet in the optical area and an employee from there had brought it back to her. Though it was obviously her fault, she left the store embarrassed without apologizing to anyone for her behavior and error.

An officer checked a license plate and it returned to a stolen vehicle. He maneuvered and attempted to find the car, but they just happened to turn into a complex and unknowingly eluded him. My partner and I were out riding bicycles and decided given the proximity of the stolen car that we would dump our bikes in the police room and drive over to the area where the stolen car was last seen. My partner turned onto a street after we got underway, and I yelled "There it is!" When I saw the stolen vehicle in the left lane of the opposite direction, we U-turned, and I informed the dispatcher of our location and travel direction. Two other officers soon joined us, and we were ready for the take down. As we switched on our lights to pull them over, one of the police cruisers decided he wasn't close enough to the action and violated S.O.P. by jerking his car around ours and angled himself in front of the suspect vehicle. By the way the felony arrest was done, we all violated S.O.P. and jumped from our vehicles and rushed the suspect vehicle, weapons at the ready, shouting "Get your hands up!" No suspect ran. We ordered the three suspects from the car and handcuffed them. The driver was arrested for the auto theft. Having no warrants, the two passengers were released. One of them was just released from jail five days before and hadn't had sufficient time to acquire any new charges.

On May 16, 1994, I had been out of the Police Academy for less than 4 years. A few other officers and me were chosen from our patrol division to participate in a Police Memorial Day Ceremony held at the Dallas City Hall Plaza. We were all there to honor and pay tribute to the several dozens of Dallas Police Officers that had died in the line of duty.

Present were the usual dignitaries like the Mayor and some council members, the Police Chief, the Dallas Police Choir, the Color Guard, several police officers who were to fire the three volley rifle salute, a bugler, some bagpipers, speaker and guests, and a riderless horse on a hilltop across the street. The group of 21 officers to whom I belonged had the somber and sobering duty of individually taking turns saying loudly from our three-column formation "KILLED IN THE LINE OF DUTY SIR!" each time the name of a fallen officer was read over a microphone. The event was attended by many family members of the fallen, and I could hear some of the sobs from grieving widows and children around us when the name of the deceased officer from their family was read. After the last of the 69 fallen Dallas Police Officer names were called, a prayer was read, followed by a long minute of total silence for reflection and remembrance.

The first Dallas Officer killed in the line of duty was 102 years before back in 1892. Of the total of 69, 10 of those had perished during my short 4-year tenure with the Dallas Police Department.

I think all the officers in attendance returned to our duties that day with a heightened awareness, perhaps with the thought on our minds that caution is not cowardice, and carelessness is not courage.

A woman married a man from Ecuador, and for the last 6 months he had been sending $1000 back there each month so that his daughter could attend private school. Now he told his American wife that he would also be sending back $500 each month so that his mother could make her house payments. His wife told him that was enough, he needed to start taking care of her, and not everybody back home. Enraged at her audacity, he grabbed her by her hair and pulled her to the ground. He delivered swift kicks to her head, face, stomach, and left ankle, and she suffered two broken fingers from trying to shield her face and head. Her husband was not present but would eventually be arrested for Aggravated Assault, but I sensed that despite having been beaten by her husband, she would drop the charges. She seemed uninterested in his going to jail and possibly face deportation.

A 12-year-old girl walked into her kitchen when the back door opened. In walked a male stranger. The stranger seemed startled to see her and asked if he could have a glass of water. She replied yes and he just helped himself to a glass, then walked into the living room. He was about to sit down on a soft chair when the cat that had been sitting there got up to move. The man grabbed the cat by the throat and held it up level with his face. The frightened girl told him that the cat was afraid of strangers, and he put the cat down. The man was sweating profusely, so the girl asked him if he needed to use the bathroom or if he needed an Advil. He told her no and to sit down. The petrified girl asked first if she could call her mom, and then also if she could walk her dog, but the man reminded her to just sit down. The girl told him the lie that her dad was due home any minute, and this caused him to stand up and walk to her bedroom. He turned to her and asked "How do I get out of here? Where's the door?" She pointed, and he walked out with the empty water glass in his hand, then she called the police. He was found a short time later when others had called the police about him at a Gas Station, where he had fondled a woman and had entered an unlocked vehicle and stole something. Mentally unbalanced presumedly from drugs, he was arrested for Burglary, Assault, and Burglary of a Motor Vehicle.

A man saw a suspect inside of a co-worker's vehicle. He ran back to the office to have the receptionist call the police, then went back outside with some co-workers to confront the car burglar, who was already walking away. The witness and his friends tried to stop the criminal from leaving until he pulled out a knife and lunged toward one of them. They still followed, but from a distance, though one of them held onto the suspect's denim jacket long enough for the suspect to pull out of it and run away. I was searching for the suspect and was flagged down by one of the witnesses who told me that the suspect ran toward the train station by running down the tracks. I had the car owner and a witness in my car who spotted the suspect sitting on a bench at the RR station. I apprehended the suspect just as he stepped onto the train and had him step back out onto the platform. One of the witnesses who had the knife pulled on him recognized it when I removed it from the suspects front right pant pocket. The witnesses identified him as their perpetrator, and he actually claimed the blue denim jacket that had been yanked off him as he ran down the tracks to the train station.

I was walking toward the door of a convenience store to go inside and get a cold drink on this 100-degree day and locked eyes with a homeless male leaning up against the brick wall about 15 yards away. I believed that the sight of me would compel him to not solicit customers for money and maybe leave the premises. I finished my refreshing drink and stepped back outside and heard someone shout "Officer! Officer!" I turned to see a man laboring to support the homeless male who looked to be on the verge of passing out. I went over and asked what was wrong with him and smelled the stench of alcohol on his breath and handcuffed him. The arrestee tried to talk to me but could only mumble unintelligibly as he unknowingly spit dried cracker crumbs in my face. I walked him over to my squad car and leaned him on my hood as I searched him. He had no ID, just $1 and a small package of crackers. I managed to cajole him into giving me his name and DOB before his whole body went limp just after he was seat belted in the backseat. I think the heat caused this drunk's ingested alcohol to metabolize faster than he expected, and he was also dehydrated. He was still unconscious when we arrived at Detox and a few soft slaps to his face would not rouse him. I hoisted him and tried to get him to support his weight as he walked, but he was all dead weight and his feet dragged. I had another officer watch him lie on the concrete ramp to the door as I quickly went inside and returned with a wheelchair. I placed his motionless body into the chair and had to hold the back of his shirt collar to keep his head and torso from falling forward as I pushed him inside. I rolled him into the small male holdover cage where he was kept for a few minutes while he waited his turn for processing. I had to face him toward the chain-link and a metal pole so that he could rest his dipping head and I applied the wheelchair brake to stabilize him. While he was unconscious, snot was oozing and dribbling from his nose onto his pants. I wheeled him out when they were ready for him, and a City Marshal Officer lifted the now barely conscious male by his left arm while I hoisted him to his feet by lifting his right arm. As he was being searched, a puddle began to form at his feet, getting larger and larger. I had to back up to avoid getting urine on my shoes.

An officer had stopped a red-light violator when a woman slowed down to tell him that there were 4 naked drunk males at a restaurant across the street. He drove over there and found 3 males glaring at him and the fourth ran into the restaurant upon seeing him. All were clothed, but didn't know that he had requested cover. I arrived with two other officers. A waiter said that the 4 drunken college students were loud and obnoxious and were spilling beer on each other from beer cans they had brought inside. We were not aware of any criminal violations other than public intoxication. We were preparing to run them to Detox when a witness told us that one of the drunks had ripped off the sunroof of a car in the parking lot and stole a radar detector from inside. The witness was driving by and about to enter the parking lot when he made this observation. Then a couple walking to their car discovered that their car had also been burglarized. While searching the suspect vehicle, I found the reported stolen property, as well as a small cedar wood box that contained marijuana and rolling papers. All the suspects admitted to drinking and smoking weed. Of the 4 arrestees that we almost took to Detox, only one now went and the 3 others went to the county jail. The fecklessness and recklessness of these irresponsible youth received a harsh dose of reality that day.

In the 1990's, homosexuality was still a taboo topic for most Americans, including Texans. The practice was widely viewed as sexual deviance. In Texas, and probably in other states, there was actually a M/C ticket charge of "Homosexual Conduct" in the Texas Penal Code for an act like kissing or even holding hands, though even then it was rarely enforced due to an expected outcry from that community. Because many gay males had no gathering place, somehow public park restrooms began to attract them. Sometimes just a few, sometimes there were many, with cars parked in the parking lot and men coming and going into the restrooms and even the woods. Some would scrawl and write lewd messages and their phone numbers on the bathroom stalls where they would have sex. They would have sex in the woods too. Day and night. From time to time the Dallas PD Vice Unit would have to work the parks, in effect being bait to make Public Lewdness arrests to thwart or slow the tide of often brazen sexual activities in the parks. Surprisingly about half of those arrested were married men caught up in the dragnet. It was a different time, when many men chose to hide their homosexuality and bisexuality.

I was one of the original two bicycle officers at White Rock Lake in Dallas, though I only did it for about a year then back in 1992. I was the only police officer assigned to the lake to assist the three Park Rangers there. That summer I worked undercover in the park for Public Lewdness prevention.

One hot and humid afternoon, my undercover partner and I decided to try one more time, as we had zero arrests that day. It was already 3:30 p.m., so if we couldn't make an arrest in 20 minutes, we would be going back to the station for quitting time at 4 p.m. My partner dropped me off on a side street to be covert, then I walked down into the park. He drove into the park to sit in his car and wait for me in the unlikely event that I could make a quick arrest.

As I walked down into the park, a young guy on a bicycle went by on the interior park street. He saw me and did a double take to see if I was headed toward the public park restroom. When he was sure that I was, the shirtless bicyclist in shorts circled back and quickly pulled his bicycle beside the stone restroom wall and walked inside. As I passed the front of the restroom on my way to the entrance, I noticed him hungrily staring at me from an open window. I walked in and saw him against the far wall, so I leaned against the wall at the entrance. I began some small talk and cupped my hands over my crotch. My right hand was over my left hand, and I started squeezing my left hand with my right hand. But in his mind, I was squeezing something else. The dude glanced down at my mid-section. I removed my hands and placed them at the small of my back. This suggestive motion was too much for the guy to remain still, and he couldn't resist temptation. With little pause, he walked forward and touched me on the outside of my pants with one with his fingertips. With no hesitation, the next moment I parried his arm away and lifted my shirt to reveal my waist clipped badge. He had the shock of his life when I said "Dallas Police! You're under arrest!" He shrank back to the rear wall in utter disbelief and horror. "No, please, just let me go, all I did was touch you, please, I'm not even a citizen, I'm a student at SMU, they'll deport me! Please just let me go!" I informed him that I couldn't do that, that he was under arrest for Public Lewdness and he needed to put his hands behind his back. He did not comply. I attempted to put his hands behind his back, but he was so sweaty that I couldn't get a grip. He unhurriedly walked outside with a dour look on his face in a state of disbelief. I tried to grasp him again, but his sweaty arms just slipped through my hands. My partner now saw me struggling to apprehend the suspect and came running. He arrived just after the suspect buckled to the ground, having collapsed under my weight of jumping on his back. The suspect was now crying, saying please, asking for somebody to please help him. In his panic-stricken emotional state, he kept kicking me as I was atop his back to handcuff him.

Before we took him to jail, we took his bike into protective custody, and he had calmed down enough so that he could talk to his sister on our car phone while I held it to his ear. I had to talk to her because he was playing dumb with her by saying he didn't do anything to get himself arrested.

A middle-aged woman was walking near an apartment complex office when she was approached by what she thought to be a 12-year-old boy and a 10-year-old girl. They told her to give them her money, but she refused. Irked by her refusal, they now loudly demanded that she give them her money, but again she refused. The 10-year-old girl clutched and tugged on the woman's purse and demanded that the purse be given to her, as did the 12-year-old boy. After tugging and tussling, the disgusted 12-year-old let go of it, but then rushed over to a landscaped edging stone retaining wall. He picked up the 5-pound pink brick and walked back to their intended victim and demanded her money or he was going to hit her with the brick. The frightened woman ran twenty yards and frantically banged on the front door of a downstairs neighbor. The man opened his door to her with her two pursuers standing just behind her. She nervously told him in broken English what had happened. The two boys made up a lame diversionary story about how a man had taken their $20 and they were just trying to get money from her to get it back. Not believing them, the man told the boys to wait there and he would call the police to help them. Of course, they wanted no part of that and fled. About 20 minutes later I already had all the information that I needed for my Attempted Aggravated Robbery report and set out to scour the neighborhood for these juvenile suspects. I had their clothing description. The girl had messy, uncombed vertical hair. I quickly found the two suspects walking down a sidewalk with several friends. I detained them and by radio had the other officer retrieve the complainant and witness and he brought them to my location for positive suspect identification. It took me several minutes to realize the supposed girl was actually a boy with a short ponytail. Positive ID was made of the suspects, who were aged 12 and 14. They were arrested, and hours later after the paperwork completion they were brought to the

Juvenile Detention Center. After having such a vile attitude with the complainant, they had been very cooperative and respectful to us. It was their first arrest. As I left them, I told the delinquents to learn from this, and that I didn't ever want to see them again if they knew what I meant. "Yes sir. Thank you, sir."

  Besides attending to major and minor crimes, police officers also respond to public safety issues, in this case a couple of dogs in the park. On a slow Autumn Day, I took it upon myself to summon Animal Control for the dogs, one large and one medium. They had been running around the park for several days. Both crossbreeds or mutts had no collars and were friendly. While I waited, I watched them run and play together, nip at each other, play wrestle. When one walked into the lake to lap up some water, the other inevitably followed. When the dog catcher arrived, the dogs sensed that something was wrong. They were not so loving anymore and skittish, but in short order the dog catcher had picked each of them up by the body and the scruff from the back of their neck and after a few yelps they were placed safely in separate cages in the back of the truck. They were both adult dogs and I hoped that they would find new homes, and that I didn't condemn a couple of playful, fun-loving dogs to death for just frolicking in the park.

An 18-year-old male had been seen loitering on a Bible Church grounds several times in a couple of months. The intuitive, dutiful Head Pastor decided that the teen may be troubled and in need of spiritual guidance, so to become his brother's keeper he tried to befriend the young man. The teenager showed up for service one Sunday, and the Pastor happened to see him and introduced him to several churchgoers. The teen pulled up his sleeves and the Pastor happened to get a good look at a tattoo that he didn't know was there, and then had to excuse himself because he had other obligations. The teen walked out to the parking lot and noticed a pre-pubescent girl reading a book in a van. She had not been feeling good and had gone outside to wait for her family until the service had ended. The 18-year-old walked over to the van, slid open the sliding door, then entered and attacked the poor little girl, ripping her shirt off. He forced the screaming and kicking girl into the back seat, digitally penetrated and then raped her. When her nightmare was over and her rapist fled, she stepped out of the van and screamed and cried continuously. The police were called, and a female officer was requested to take the report. I never did see the victim, as the officer was with the victim and her mother behind a closed door. The Pastor gave me the suspect name and the tattoo description and said the suspect had told him of a pending case he had in Dallas for drug possession. The rapist's father was in a Texas jail for beating someone with a baseball bat, and his mother had kicked him out of her apartment.

The girl was brought to Children's Hospital for an examination, and her clothes were brought to the Physical Evidence Section. The next day, the girl identified the suspect from a photo lineup.

A Channel 5 reporter was interviewing me about citations written at White Rock Lake as I sat on my bicycle. A bicyclist stopped and told me that an abandoned vehicle was back around the corner and left in the middle of the road. He saw a couple nearby that might've been drunk. I turned my bicycle around and rode off with the news cameraman filming me. Two blocks away, I stopped alongside the vehicle and peered inside, but the car was empty. I looked around for the occupants and a couple of helpful fishermen pointed to a spot at the edge of the river. I walked over and saw that a male and female were cooling off by swimming in the river, laughing and enjoying themselves. They hadn't bothered to remove any of their clothes, and apparently didn't care about the need to replace their left rear tire which was shredded down to the rim. They had left a metal can of toluene on the grass between them and their car which reeked of that odor when I opened the door to shut off the car ignition. I found no alcohol, but they had intoxicated themselves by inhaling paint thinner fumes. I had them come ashore, and asked for their ID. The female didn't have any, but the male did. He removed his soaked wallet from his rear pants pocket and handed me his ID. Two losers, both around 30 years old. She had been handled before for burglary. Both went to Detox and were listed as suspects in a separate report I did for having found a counterfeit $100 bill atop their dashboard prior to towing their vehicle.

It was late December 2000, and I was working a Violent Crime Task Force for overtime. We had to generate our own activity and try to put someone in jail. I spied a vehicle pull out quickly from an apartment complex and I rushed to try to run the tag, but then saw another officer had already positioned himself behind that car. Before I could turn to follow them, I had to wait for a car to pass by. When it did, I checked that tag and found warrants, so now I changed plans and decided to stop this vehicle. The other officer and I both did a traffic stop on our motorists at the same restaurant parking lot, me on one drive and him on the other. My subject with the warrants wasn't in the car, so I cut the driver loose and circled my car to cover the other officer. Two more officers arrived. One of them smelled freshly smoked crack cocaine, so we had all 3 males step out of the car. The driver would be going to jail for a DWI warrant. An officer searching their vehicle found some rocks of crack cocaine under the front passenger seat, so the suspect that had been sitting there was handcuffed. He was perplexed and couldn't understand why he was being charged with drug possession because it wasn't his car. Rather than try to parlay that into a possible "Not Guilty" verdict at his trial, like so many unthinking criminals he didn't think about the consequences of his actions. He was just released from jail and just knew that he didn't want to return. He dashed off, cuffed hands behind his back. I followed him but didn't have to pursue him for long. The arrestee slipped on some gravel about 20 yards into his mad dash and took a header onto the rear chrome fender of a Pick-Up truck. His forward momentum had placed him partly under the truck, so I grabbed his legs and yanked him out. He was bleeding from a laceration above his right eye. Paramedics arrived to examine him. He eventually went to the hospital from the County jail, determined by the jail nurse to need X-rays and stitches. I was sure that he regretted his impetuous decision, because besides the drug charge, he was charged with Felony Escape for his futile escape attempt.

A boss terminated a man one morning and then went back to clear out whatever items the ex-employee didn't take from his desk. There he found a calendar that had disturbing writings, such as "What is light without the darkness, what is good without evil? Lord, grant me the power to control my temper. Grant me the knowledge to hide and dispose of the bodies of the people who PISS ME OFF!" The fired employee had told a co-worker that he was a Satan worshipper. He had also threatened to cut another employee's throat a month earlier (don't know why he wasn't fired then). The boss was going to hire an armed security guard for a week so that his employees felt safe.

A woman assisted a traveling veterinarian who euthanized pets at house calls. She brought her dementia-afflicted husband with her and left him seat belted in the car in front of a client's home, leaving her key in the ignition so that her husband could listen to the radio. When her somber task was completed, she stepped outside to find that her car and husband were both gone. Her boss drove her to our station, where I was just starting my shift. I obtained info about the vehicle and her husband and told her that because of his diminished mental capacity from dementia, a Critical Missing report would be made and police would be searching for him constantly until he was found. The woman didn't have her purse nor her phone because she had left her purse on the backseat of the missing car. She was fortunate to remember her sisters phone number who I had send me a picture of her missing brother-in -law to my cell phone. I forwarded that picture to a few other officers, and to a Sergeant who would send it to his email, then make a photocopy for distribution on the next shift which began in one and in two hours. It was raining, our complainant hadn't driven in a while, and he was 30 miles from his home. He was unfamiliar with the area, but in his mental state that could really be said about anywhere. We were working with our Fusion Unit to issue a statewide Silver Alert to all police agencies and known cell phones across the state. Just one hour from when I started to take the report, the sister phoned me to report that her brother-in-law was safe. He had driven 30 miles to a small town 7-Eleven. The clerk postulated that he was lost and confused and needed help, because he struggled to speak but couldn't make his destination or desires known. The responding officer found the wife's purse on the rear seat, and called the last dialed number on the phone which was the sister. The sister drove to the 7-Eleven to retrieve him, and then to a shopping center store parking lot 20 miles away from me so that I could reunite the anxious wife with her husband. They were lucky because with his driving the situation could have been catastrophic.

A late-night element (unit) had arrested a drunk male for banging on the wrong door during a torrential downpour and now needed a day shift officer to transport him to Detox. I was taking him there, and along the way he mentioned that he had no ID and didn't have any papers. To clarify, I asked him if he was here illegally, and he admitted that he was. I jokingly asked him if he would rather go back to Mexico than to go to where we put drunk people. His eyes lit up, and he became very animated. "Si! Si! You take me to Mexico? Si Senor! Yes. Thank you, officer! Thank You! I go to Mexico! Ha! Ha!" I phoned my Sgt., who said if it was okay with INS (which became ICE), that'd be fine. I phoned them and they had no problem with it, instructing me to just drop him off by their office. We arrived with plenty of time for him to board the Friday bus. Another happy customer.

I turned into a parking lot at the lake and got behind a vehicle parked in a handicapped space with no handicapped license plate or rear-view mirror placard showing. I approached the seated driver who was talking on her phone. She asked me if something was wrong, and I asked if she had a handicapped placard. She said that she had just pulled in and parked there, and could she get a warning and just move it? This befuddled me because there were several open parking spaces in the small lot, but she chose a clearly marked handicapped spot with marked pavement and a big sign in front of her car. I told her that she must think it is okay to park in a handicapped spot until she is caught by the police. I wasn't going to give her a warning and said that she deserved a ticket. She called her husband on the phone to tell him that I was rude. I was unsurprised by the young woman's attitude. For far too many people, when an officer writes them a ticket, he is rude, but when the officer gives them a warning, he is nice.

It was 9:30 p.m., just before I was to end my shift at 10. I noticed a full parking lot in a small park adjacent to White Rock Lake that should be nearly empty at this hour. I decided to investigate, knowing that there was a good chance that my patrol car would not be seen in the dimly lit lot, and that people in the park had a tree obstructed view of the parking lot. I placed myself on a temporary mark out at this park address, then surprised a couple of High School kids drinking alcohol and wrote two tickets. When I asked them, they informed me that the group down below was about fifty High School thespian kids, which raised no red flags in my mind for my safety. I brought my ticket book with me as I walked down the darkened winding sidewalk that descended to their area, just happening to approach them from behind while they were all facing forward listening to an outdoor "Poetry Slam" in the dark. After each reading, all the audience members would snap their fingers several times to show equal appreciation. It was obvious that these kids all thought that inserting some variation of the F-bomb into their poems was cool, the more the better. I thought that using that word showed stupidity, but then I was no student "poet." I wanted to tell them all that profanity was not profound, but I was too busy writing tickets to minors who were holding and drinking beer while I picked them off one by one in the dark from behind. At some point the presence of a police officer amid this uncrowded crowd became more widely known. Some 12 and 24 packs of beer were being abandoned on the pavement as the students became more dispersed around me. There were still a few unaware of my presence that received a ticket, as did an unthinking bonehead that decided he was going to salvage one of the unattended open 24 packs of beer. When there were no more Minor in Possession tickets to be written and the element of surprise had passed, I just stood there listening to the poetry performances pretending to be hanging onto their every word. The kids were chattering quietly about why didn't I just leave. I knew that if I did, the drinking would continue until the poetry party was over and it was time for the kids to get back into their mom and dad's vehicle to drive somewhere else or go home. I played the waiting game, and they blinked first. It wasn't long before the partiers had left, and the kids who just wanted a simple poetry slam remained. Some told me they had told people to not bring alcohol, but some didn't listen, and some unknown kids with alcohol from other schools had started to appear before I arrived. The drinkers having departed, I left too.

At midnight, two friends in a car stopped at a red light. From each side simultaneously came a male suspect wearing all black including ski masks. The suspect on the driver side pointed a .38 pistol at them and announced, "This is a carjacking!" The two friends got out of the car as told, but then were told to get into the back seat because a car was approaching from behind. The two friends hunkered in fear on the back seat while the two suspects up front mostly whispered in a sometimes-intense quarrel. The car stopped in a remote, unlit wooded area of a Dallas suburb. The two who were kidnapped were ordered to get out of their car, and then were beaten with punches and kicks. One was punched twice in the stomach, and when he buckled over in pain, he received a pistol whip to the back of his head and was unconscious for two hours. When he regained consciousness, his friend was at his side and the suspects were long gone with their vehicle. The two friends walked several miles to one of their homes, and one set of parents brought their son to a hospital ER for safety concerns about a possible concussion, where they also called the police. I told them that given the crime, the time of the crime, the heated discussion between the suspects, and the remote location to which their son was driven that the subject of execution was likely discussed.

An officer was responding to a Burglary-in-progress call when he and the burglar surprised each other. The suspect aimed and fired his Tec-9 machine pistol at the officer once but missed. The officer returned fire twice, missing the suspect once but striking him with the second gunshot in the right thigh. The suspect tossed his weapon over a fence, and then surmounted that fence like his injury was no hindrance at all. The suspect ran down and along a creek bed and ended up being captured by other officers a couple hundred yards away. After he was treated at a hospital, the arrestee was transported by me and another officer downtown to be interviewed by some CAPERS (Crimes Against Persons) Detectives. We parked in the basement of the old Police HQ, the same parking lot where Jack Ruby shot and killed John F. Kennedy's assassin, Lee Harvey Oswald in 1963. We soon discovered that there was no wheelchair for our wounded arrestee, so we decided to support him as best as we could by each placing an arm under each of his shoulders to make the trip to the office. We had made him lighter on his feet, but his struggle to walk was not effortless. What little pressure he had applied on his bad leg while being supported by us was still enough to reopen his wound. The arrestee noticed and felt blood dripping down his leg. We located some bathroom paper towels to soak up his blood drops and the pool of blood that now formed on the floor at his stationary feet. It was obvious we had to make alternate travels plans. We found a swivel chair on wheels. I outfitted it with a clear plastic cleaner's sheet cover that I found in the trash to protect it from any bleeding, then wheeled him to the elevator and to his interview destination.

A 13-year-old boy was walking his two dogs on a narrow grassy strip between a fence and a parking lot on a cool December day. Some unknown teenagers jumped him from behind and one of them pulled his jacket up over his head. The victim was then beaten amidst shouts of "Get him! Jump him! Kick him! Hit him! Punk! Mark!" (I learned that was slang for punk).

His two dogs barked but neither of them protected him.

Citizens occasionally walk up to police officers and start a conversation, often preceded by gratitude for what we do. A woman in her 60's walked over to me and began a conversation in the same manner. She mentioned that she was from

Wisconsin, and I commented that I was from north of Chicago. She went on to say that "there was a serial killer by the name of Gaines or something from near where she grew up. Police had finally caught up to him and went to explore his house with a warrant. They found a blood trail and followed it to a barn, where a young woman was hanging upside down like a deer, with her limbs strung up. Her belly had been sliced open where he had pulled out her insides and her heart. When the police went inside of the house, they found jars of body parts and organs on the sides of the stairs. The smell must have been awful because his mother had died a while ago and he had left her body upstairs."

She felt the need to tell me this story while I was in a restaurant at the time of her interruption, trying to eat my salad that had red house dressing on it.

My Patrol Division had some overtime money available one December earmarked for a Violent Crime Task Force. The name was deceiving. Though we were expected to respond to violent crime calls, in the cold of December nights crime was not rampant and around every corner. If 911 calls involving violent crimes were absent, then we were to generate activity by being proactive, like checking suspicious people or making traffic stops to find people with warrants.

Knowing that the call load would be low, my partner and I were assigned to patrol a small territory of about 15 apartment complexes between our hours of 9 p.m.-3 a.m. It was hoped that we would be fortunate enough to catch someone in the act of breaking into a car, but we knew of the astronomical odds against that. After about 4 hours of patrol boredom at those apartments, we decided to take a 10- minute drive to White Rock Lake Park and write some past park curfew violation tickets, giving us probable cause to check the violators for any outstanding warrants and make a trip to jail to be productive. I spotted a small, parked vehicle near a closed-for-the-winter public restroom immediately upon entering the park and directed my spotlight at the occupant. He was slumped unconscious over his steering wheel, or maybe he was dead. He wasn't moving, and both front windows were more than halfway down in sub-40-degree weather. We exited our vehicle and walked toward him, shining our flashlights on his head. When I reached the driver side, I could see that he had passed out drunk because a nearly empty quart bottle of Schlitz Malt Liquor lay next to him. He also had his pants pulled down to his knees with his hands on his lap, and one hand partly on his exposed penis. I shook him awake and had him pull up his pants. We arrested him for Public Intoxication. He also received tickets for Park Curfew violation and possession of alcohol in a city park.

I received a dispatched call about a domestic disturbance from a neighbor who chose not to be contacted. As I was arriving, the other officer who was already at the apartment door told me by radio to go to the office for a key to the apartment. He had heard an argument when he first arrived, but after he knocked and alerted them by saying "Police", everything went quiet. I brought a key, but it didn't fit; the tenant had apparently changed the lock but had not provided a spare key to management, a certain lease violation. We knocked a bit more, then called for a supervisor. We apprised him of the situation and knocked on some windows too. I announced that ignoring us would not make us go away, that we needed to make sure everyone was okay before we could leave. Still no answer or noise. I stood facing the door squarely, with an officer behind me on my left and right. I stabilized myself by holding the corner of the building with my left hand, and a wooden beam with my right. I catapulted myself forward being airborne as I thrust landed well targeted kicks with my left leg. After about five kicks, I realized that this steel door was too solid, and all that I was doing was placing some black combat boot heel marks on the door. A couple of more less energetic kicks and the door suddenly opened, but not from my futile efforts. A young long-haired man on the inside opened it and said "Hey! What's going on?" as he stood there stark naked in broad daylight. I pushed past him (he was obviously unarmed and not a threat) to inspect the rest of the apartment for officer safety. I passed a young attractive woman who was standing in the middle of the apartment also naked as a jaybird. I gave her a thorough look as I continued nonstop to search the rest of the apartment. It was just this couple. One of the officers behind me had told the woman to get down on the floor. When I returned an officer told her to put a towel on. The shower was running, and they couldn't hear the door knocks, but we knew that was a lie. They were both dry. As another officer was speaking to the woman, I checked for any damage that I may have caused to the door. As I stood there, I glanced back in the living room where the pretty woman had sat on the couch. A large white towel was wrapped around her, but she had wrapped it under her bountiful breasts, not over them. She must've caught me glaring because she raised her towel to cover them. The man lied to us and said that there had been no problem there, but she was honest and said the verbal argument began after it was realized that her two Dalmatian dogs had urinated on the couch. I had the dispatcher check the male for warrants, and he had two from a suburb which were confirmed as valid. We had him put some clothes on under our watchful eye, checking the pockets of those clothes as we handed them to him and then took him downtown to jail.

A woman spoke with two young males at her front door near sunset and wrote them a check for some magazine subscriptions. She closed and locked the door behind her and laid on her bed to watch TV. Minutes later, her Saint Bernard dog started to bark nonstop for a bit, so the woman, --who was at home alone—started to think that maybe the magazine salesmen were prowling around outside. She felt safer when she pulled out a semi-automatic pistol from the nightstand drawer and placed it between her legs as she watched TV. A few minutes later she thought that she would move the pistol to her left side. She thought that she must have cocked the weapon by pulling the hammer back earlier because she unintentionally touched the trigger and the gun fired. The bullet went through the calve muscle of her left leg and lodged into the mattress. It was a Code 3 call for me. When I arrived, she was calmly sitting on her front porch talking with the attending paramedics. She said that she wasn't in much pain and had nonchalantly called her husband and 911 to report that she had accidentally shot herself. She joked that she retrieved the pistol to protect herself but never thought that she would need protection from herself. We unloaded her pistol back in the bedroom. Her husband arrived home and we instructed him to take her to the nearby hospital to avoid infection. The expense of an ambulance ride wasn't needed, as the bandaged calve would be fine until he took her there. I gave the husband the report number along with my name and phone number, since hospitals automatically called the police for all gunshot victims.

At 10:30 p.m. one night I was driving home from work in my personal car while still in uniform. I had just driven past the small downtown of where I lived when a large pick-up truck tailgated me in my little Kia. I looked down at my speedometer to be sure that I wasn't driving under the speed limit, but I was progressing along on the single lane road at the posted speed limit of 50. The tailgater started flashing his bright lights at me. After he did that several times, I found it annoying and began to tap my brake to get him to back off. Of course, the driver behind me disapproved and flashed me rapid successions of his high beams. I pulled off to the shoulder to allow him to pass. He accelerated quickly only to have to stop at a red light fifty yards down the road. Now it was my turn to show him how annoying he had been by giving him a dose of his own medicine. The light changed to green, and now I began to flicker my bright lights intermittently. He slowed down and braked just as I had, then he slowly drove and slowed down to pull over to the shoulder as he rolled down his window. Simultaneously, he leaned out and down to be sure that I saw him giving me the middle finger.

I pulled alongside him and lowered my passenger window to be sure that he saw me when I leaned over toward him and said, "Hey! If you want to talk about this then pull over into the parking lot!" Seeing my police uniform, his single finger greeting disappeared quickly and he responded with a "No", adding that he didn't want to go to jail. The approximately 20-year-old driver felt so big and powerful sitting up high in Daddy's Pick-up truck, but I shriveled him back down to a meek size. I wondered how many times he let his testosterone-fueled condescension intimidate other drivers? It felt good to intimidate the intimidator.

I responded to a call where a woman simply wanted me to create a written record in case something happened to her 21-year-old daughter and her two grandsons. The woman had allowed them to stay with her for two months, but now a voodoo priestess who had been steadily gaining her daughter's trust and confidence had come to retrieve them and her few suitcases to come and live with her. The woman was convinced that this witch had a psychological hold on her daughter and was fearful of what her daughter may be persuaded to do in her nuanced trance. Others had told this woman that the black magic practitioners' house was not a place for children. One room was reportedly painted all black with numerous candles.

The witch had been seen to sprinkle powders and mix strange concoctions, and supposedly paid people cash when they brought her black cats. Some truth mixed with rumors, I'm sure.

My partner and I were concealed in a wooded area, observing suspicious activity in an adjacent public park parking lot. A male pulled into a space front forward. Minutes later, another vehicle drove into the lot and the driver backed his car up so that the two driver doors were adjacent. The two men flirted for several minutes. Then the man in the vehicle closest to us stepped out so that the other man could get a better look at what he looked like from the waist down, using his driver door as a shield from any viewer on the non-wooded side. It was mid-day in a public park and the only article of clothing this guy was wearing was a shirt. Moments later, an unwelcome van pulled into the parking lot and Mr. Pant-less quickly entered his car to avoid detection. Soon the second vehicle departed, leaving our "flasher" with the van driver. But he wasn't interested in the van male, so he vacated the lot too. My partner and I scrambled through the woods to get back to our unseen squad car so that we could get to the park and pull over Mr. Pant-less. We rushed and drove around to the nearest intersection. We knew his license plate and spotted him, maneuvering to be behind him. We flipped on our emergency lights for a traffic stop, but he hadn't had a chance to put his pants on so he wasn't pulling over, trying to buy time to somehow get dressed while he drove. I got on the mic for the loudspeaker and ordered him to pull over. He still ignored us and piddled along. I spoke into the mic again with a stern "Pull your car over right now!" and he complied. Before he could clothe himself, we were rapidly at his doors. He only had a chance to put his blue jeans atop his lap and was quite embarrassed. We did what we could to cause him to feel ashamed, doing what he did in a public park where women and children could be present. He received a ticket for "Disorderly Conduct--Obscene display", and we never saw him again.

I saw a teenaged boy cross the street while I was driving through a residential neighborhood. I called him over and stepped out of my car. Placing him against my cruiser, I patted him down then told him to get in the car because I was taking him to school. He told me that he used to go to the school where I was taking him, but that he currently attended an alternative school. I told him that I'm not going to take his word for it and would confirm it in the school office. We entered the school and an Assistant Principal happened to be in the hallway. He told me that the boy indeed attended an alternative school. He placed the boy in what I assumed to be a secure office and closed the door because he wanted to talk to me. We walked several yards to the hallway where he informed me that the truant was believed to have a probation violation. I asked him to get the kid's true name and DOB in case he had lied to me. From peripheral vision I detected movement at the end of the hallway, where some kid had dashed out an interior door and then hustled outside into the portable classroom area. I commented to the Assistant Principal that I just saw another kid ditch school, and he speculated that it was probably just some kid that was late for his portable classroom. I received the correct info on my truant and stepped back into the office to call the Youth Division to verify that this kid had a warrant. The kid was gone! Then I saw that the kid had exited through a side door of the office, then through the front office, and out the door that led to the portables. The principal broadcasted on his radio to his maintenance people and truant officers to be on the lookout for this kid. One reported back that the juvenile was walking down the RR track behind the school. I rushed out to my car and drove around the corner, where the truant and I saw each other simultaneously. He started running and I drove to parallel him. He reversed course and I left my car to follow him in a foot pursuit. I tried to tell the dispatcher that I was "On the ground ", but apparently did not transmit. The pursuit took me through a grassy ditch, across a road, and onto white stones along the RR track. As we ran along this track, the kid kept glancing over his shoulder to see where I was instead of focusing on where he was stepping to be sure of his footing. This 42-year-old officer caught up to the 14-year-old kid and shoved him from behind for balance displacement, and he fell to the rocks on which we were running. I had to force his arms behind his back to cuff him, and then hoisted him to his feet. As I led him back to my squad car, I was holding him high on his toes by pulling up on the scruff on the back of his shirt. Four school employees were waiting near my squad car as we returned and one of them gave me a glint of pride over my apprehension when he smiled and said, "Good job officer".

I took the kid to Youth for his probation violation and the Detective was surprised that I was going to charge the kid with Evading Detention, saying it was more trouble than it was worth and like too many criminal charges against juveniles would simply be another probated case. I agreed, and the kid was just charged with his Probation Violation for Robbery.

Calls to 911 aren't always accurate. They are sometimes excited exaggerations, or misunderstandings by the 911 clerk or caller. I was going to a call that made me a little apprehensive. There were supposed to be about 30 males in the park fighting with baseball bats. I only had one way to approach from a wide baseball diamond parking lot so everyone could see me coming. Dozens of people--mostly men--scattered and walked away to their vehicles as I approached. Not one of them had a bat in their hands. Then a couple pointed at a vehicle that passed me going in the other direction and told me that they were the ones who were fighting. Stopping the suspects is always paramount before they have a chance to escape. The details and facts could wait. I U-turned and pulled them over into a parking space. I learned from others that one baseball team had been enjoying a lopsided lead a bit too much and started showing bad sportsmanship by getting cocky, insulting, and boastful. The fans of the losing team didn't care for their antics and some heated words were exchanged, then some beer bottles were thrown. No one was struck by the projectiles. The driver that I stopped was one of the instigators of the bottle tossing. I wrote him a couple traffic tickets, for No DL and No Insurance. A team manager said that they were only in the 5th inning but because of the fracas the remainder of the game was cancelled by the umpire. Few people left when he did this, and even now few vehicles were leaving the parking lot despite the game being over and two police officers being present. I thought that there had to be a reason why they mostly remained. Sure enough, when I wandered around the parking lot, I found what could be described as their beer truck. There were five cases of Corona bottles and Bud Light cans of beer in the bed of a PU truck, but no one was near it. I asked aloud for an owner, but no one wanted the $150 ticket for illegally possessing alcohol in a city park. We emptied every bottle and beer can which ended the loitering of vehicles and they now all left en masse. There would be no postgame drinking. The unknown vehicle owner returned sometime after we departed to reclaim his vehicle.

I observed two cars parked alongside each other in a part of a park called "Flagpole Hill". This area occasionally had couples going there for sex, usually homosexuals. I parked my car and quietly walked to the two cars and thought they were empty, but then I noticed movement in the backseat of the Pick-Up truck with tinted windows. A woman's head had risen and she was now sitting upright. I shifted my attention to the back seat and pressed my hand against the tinted glass to peer inside and saw that woman's head had been in the lap of a man who had his pants down and had an erect penis. It was obvious that fellatio had occurred, but I didn't see it, so there could be no arrest for Public Lewdness. He pulled up his pants, and they both stepped out of the truck. I wrote him a citation for Obscene Display/Conduct. Having checked their license plates, I saw different names and addresses as well as them both wearing wedding rings. I commented that I knew that they were both married but not to each other. They had no remarks. The man simply inferred his desire to be discreet by asking me "Where can I go to pay for this?"

Officers were dispatched on a call involving a teenaged blonde girl who was seen stealing a bicycle from a garage. Minutes later another citizen reported a suspicious blue van driving slowly thru the neighborhood just blocks ways. Our Deployment team reacted quickly by announcing that it was believed that the same van had been used in many local thefts and burglaries. I spotted a blue van in the distance when I reached the general area and I raced to catch up to it to ascertain if it was our suspect vehicle. As I marked out on traffic, I could see that there was a blonde girl inside the van as well as a bicycle visible via the rear door windows. Other officers were quickly on the scene, and we had all of the van occupants step out and place their hands on the side of the van as we patted them down for safety. The bicycle was returned to the owners. Being recent immigrants, they didn't want to get involved in the criminal justice system and were happy to get their bicycle returned by the police but were uninterested in having the blonde burglar prosecuted. A couple of van occupants were transported by us to our Investigative unit to be interrogated about this and other thefts and burglaries. The driver had been driving at the time of the offense but also needed to be interviewed. After placing two sets of hand cuff on the wrists of the unwieldy, obese, inflexible 340 lb. suspect his sweaty body was sandwiched into my front passenger seat. Though he was only in his early 30's he'd had a triple bypass just three weeks earlier and soon was breathing heavily. He appeared to be on the verge of becoming unconscious, so I radioed for an ambulance. It was a chore to jockey and lift him back out of the car for his walk to the ambulance, his knees nearly buckling under the crushing weight of his body. He escaped his ticket warrants for now. There were no witnesses to place him at the scene of the bicycle burglary, though the case detective would probably file some theft and burglary charges on him "At Large" for other crimes in which he was involved pending the other suspects and witnesses' cooperation.

A 26-year-old woman walked into a home improvement store with a completed credit card application in hand. An employee contacted the credit bureau and was informed that the personal information on their application was fraudulent but to go ahead and issue her a trackable, temporary credit and card number. The police were called, and the employee said that the suspect had been given a $50 credit limit and 10% off on any purchase she made today to stall for time. The suspect became nervous over the time spent to acquire her credit card and left the business, only to be seen going into a beauty supply business several storefronts down. I arrived and parked behind what I knew to be the accomplice's vehicle and handcuffed the male, though he was later released given his cooperation and truthfulness. The female suspect was brought out from the store and handcuffed. She had just committed a forgery inside by endorsing and tendering another woman's check for a purchase. The items that she bought were returned, and the red billfold that our arrestee had been carrying was searched. She had an altered TX DL with her picture placed inside the DL which had belonged to another woman with the other woman's name and address, as well as two check books owned by the other woman. Our arrestee also had some other ID's and social security cards belonging to other women in her billfold, but this was before there was a law making that in itself a separate criminal charge, so they were later taken to a Forgery detective to sort out. Our arrestee had none of her own ID, and so was fingerprinted/rapped out at the county jail, where it was determined that she had county and ticket warrants under her alias and her true name. From start to finish, this call took me 7 hours to process, including 5 hours of overtime. She was charged with the three felonies of Credit Card Abuse, Forgery, Counterfeit Instrument, and the misdemeanors of Fail to ID as a Fugitive and 13 county and city ticket warrants.

While patrolling White Rock Lake, a woman driving in the opposite direction flagged me down and stopped her car. She had been speaking to a 911 operator, and I heard her say "It's okay, I've got an officer now". I was told a woman not far behind her just escaped from a car and was screaming. I drove only 50 more yards and I could see and hear my complainant lamenting and sobbing, accompanied by three park patrons who had come to her aid when they first heard her shouting for help.

The ordeal began when this woman agreed to meet her boyfriend of 6 months at a restaurant parking lot. She was intending to terminate their relationship and sensed that he knew it. She had decided to perform an online criminal history check on him and was astounded and disappointed; he had gone more than a little afoul of the law. She found that he had done 20 years in prison for a felony and had just been released prior to their dating; he was not the man that she thought she knew and the news scared her. Still daylight when she arrived at the parking lot, her soon-to-be ex-boyfriend took her keys from her hand as she stepped out of her car, then sat on the driver seat and told her to get in. He wanted to visit White Rock Lake so that they could talk about things. She was disinclined to do that but when he started to reverse with her purse and phone still in her car she hopped aboard. Driving down the road he tried to talk to her, and she could detect alcohol on his breath and thought he might also be high from drugs. She persisted at her insistence that he take her back to the restaurant, and this indignity set him off. Now impatient, and not being able to manipulate her to his will, he slandered her and pulled her hair. He choked her with one hand and held her head against the passenger window and she cried for him to stop and let her out, but every time she unlocked her door, he would lock it from the driver side. When she finally succeeded, he stopped the car and grabbed hold of her left arm to yank her back inside the car. She resisted and screamed for help, gesticulating wildly with her other hand as she did. Soon, three good Samaritans were present and tugged on her right arm and won the tug of war allowing her to escape. The suspect drove off when someone said they would call the police. The victim was still wailing uncontrollably when I arrived, feeling certain that he might've killed her. I recorded the info of the witnesses then had an officer follow me and the complainant back to the restaurant in case the suspect had dropped off her car there and was lurking nearby to start her assault anew. The suspect was still driving her car, whereabouts unknown. I wrote down the suspect vehicle info, and then drove the complainant to her home 35 miles away to be certain that the suspect wasn't waiting for her and to complete a family violence packet for the report. She was very grateful for my help and felt safe for the night because her teenaged son was in the house, so she would not be alone. I told her to phone the local police if she saw the suspect outside her house.

We had been told in our morning detail that a call had been received by an anonymous attorney who said that there were some dead bodies in a small house of a neighborhood only a few blocks from the police station. The caller seemed very emotional and serious, so the call was not dismissed as a prank or hoax. Detectives began canvassing the area to speak to residents living within an adequate perimeter around the station, a methodical, tedious process that would require some luck. A woman informed her mailman that the police were concerned about the welfare of two people but didn't exactly know where they lived. The mailman told her of a house across the street that had a few days of uncollected mail, and then he visited the police station to share this information. I was starting an Assault report when I heard officers request a supervisor, Crimes Against Persons (CAPERS), the Physical Evidence Section (PES), a Medical Examiner (ME) and an ambulance. There was one 23-year-old male who was fully incapacitated, lying on a bed and left for dead. He had been bludgeoned several times on his head, giving him large open gashes, a fractured skull, and a broken arm from what was undoubtedly a defensive reflex. He was the only witness to a double homicide in the house. They had both been executed with a shot to the head. He had the misfortune of having been living at the drug house just the last two weeks. Much aware of the drug dealing and probably dealing himself, he had not been an intended target but being a witness, he became an impromptu and a presumed homicide victim by his assailants.

I had the dispatcher put me out at the location, then pushed hard to finish a lengthy report that I had already started. After completion, I walked up the driveway only to be told by a Sergeant coming down the driveway with two officers in tow that I could go ahead and leave; they were finishing up and just needed one patrol officer present while the crime scene was being processed by other police personnel.

Over the next two weeks our sole survivor was placed under guard at the hospital to heal and until his memory and clarity improved. I was a police guard at his room with another officer a few times. We were to notify Homicide if he had anybody who tried to visit him. Nobody came to see him. He was admitted by police request and for the safety of the medical staff as simply "Mr. M", which wasn't even the first letter of his last name.

A blue Honda was driven to the rear of an apartment complex and was left on the grass adjacent to the woods with the two left side doors removed and missing. No one was in the vicinity. The lower steering column had been separated and was dangling, exposing the ignition innards. The car had obviously been stolen but had not yet been reported as such by the owner. I towed the vehicle as found property so that the owner would already have it under police protection when he called. As I was nearing departure a man walked out with his two young kids and told me that his Cadillac had been stolen and that he parked it near my car in the lot. The car thieves had likely made a swap out. I took his information to make the report, and then did him the favor of taking him over to a childcare facility to drop off his kids and then took him back to his apartment. I checked with the Auto Pound and by clerical error his just stolen car still showed to be there. My owner had his Cadillac stolen 10 days earlier but retrieved it three days ago. An officer had showed his car "recovered" on the report after it was stolen, but no one had brought his car to the pound since then, and faulty paperwork still showed it to be there. He told me that shortly after taking possession of their car again, his wife found a Food Stamp Card in an envelope lying on the floorboard. The card either belonged to the suspect or an accomplice, or to the victim of another crime. I did another found property report, supplementing both my stolen Cadillac report and my Honda found property report with the additional information and placed the Food Stamp Card in the property room. Minutes before leaving that day, I checked to see what calls were in the queue and un-dispatched and there was a call at that same address involving the car owner having found some car parts.

I was riding my bicycle across a baseball field on the way to White Rock Lake when I saw a player urinating in the middle of left field during daytime. The 13-year-old had his back to the bleachers but was facing me and some houses in the distance. I rode up on him and he awkwardly tucked himself back inside his pants, but it wasn't even close to my not having seen him in the act. I had him summon his coach. The kid was smiling because his teammates knew what had happened and were snickering. It was just a practice game, and the boy could have waited until his team had gone to bat and used one of the three portable potties that were at an adjacent ball diamond. The boy's coach and father returned, and I clued them in. By the look on their faces, they took the incident seriously, but the boy was trying not to laugh and was stifling a grin, thinking it was a big joke. I told him that he should feel ashamed and embarrassed, that I didn't like his attitude, and I wrote him a urinating in public citation. The mother of the boy called the police station to complain about me to my Sergeant, but complain about what? That I enforced the law? I'm sure that she didn't think urinating in public was acceptable behavior by anyone else, but it was okay for her son? Why waste her and my Sergeant's time with a retaliatory gripe?

The co-owner of a small school cafeteria found some frozen meat in the sleeves of a Cowboy's jacket that had been left behind at the office when the jacket owner left for home without it, as the day had become much warmer at the end of her shift. When she remembered and returned to retrieve it, she plead ignorance and was reticent to confess to having done anything. She claimed that she didn't know who put the meat into her jacket sleeves. We arrived and the suspect admitted that she had been to prison before. I don't know why but the other officer had her and two other employees detained, and they removed their shoes and socks in full view of management. The primary suspect was the only one who struck her shoes together like what every jailer does during arrestee processing. During the wait for the police, the jacket owner suspect was allowed to use the cafeteria restroom. I don't know what she unloaded in there, I mean besides what the average person would. I found out later that the toilet had never clogged before, but it did after her use. I'm sure that she was terminated.

I took an alarm call at the end of my workday knowing that 98% of alarms are false so I wouldn't be long. Moments later, the dispatcher advised me that there was a 41-11 at the same address, which for us is a Burglary-in-progress. I was in the proximity when the dispatcher provided a suspect clothing description and direction of travel as he fled the scene on foot. Two blocks away I observed the suspect jogging down the bicycle trail of White Rock Lake. I stopped and detained the suspect, getting his DL. He curiously was not inquisitive as to why I was talking with him and was just silent. When I did ask where he was coming from, he said that he had been peering through the window of a stylish house under construction when he noticed that a neighbor was watching him, so he left. When I asked why if he was so innocent that he didn't just speak to the neighbor, why was he running, and if his cousin was going to pick him up then why was he wandering further away, he became perplexed and visibly nervous. When other officers arrived to cover me, I checked him for warrants, but he had none. Interestingly though upon performing a criminal history check and questioning him about it, he told me how he was acquitted after being on trial for Attempted Burglary and

Evading Detention, supposedly for a lack of evidence. I completed a Suspicious Person report; he would be a good person for our undercover deployment officers to follow in the future in the hopes of catching him in the commission of a crime.

A man phoned police to report that he had been hit on the head by an unknown suspect wielding a baseball bat. I arrived before the ambulance and saw the obese 23-year-old complainant sitting in a chair on his front porch. The right side of his forehead was covered in blood. I broadcasted a description of the suspect that had attacked him. I turned back to see a paramedic wipe the blood away from his forehead, but there was surprisingly no bruise or swelling, only three deep scratches that appeared to me to have been caused by fingernails. I looked at the complainant's fingernails and saw blood. I had thought that he had looked familiar to me and now I had the recollection. About a year ago I had taken him to a hospital psych ward because he had used a knife to scratch his wrist. To confirm my suspicions, I asked if he had been an MHMR patient before and he had been. I got back on the radio and cancelled my earlier broadcast of the fleeing suspect. He raised my ire, and I told him to not lie to the police, that another officer unfamiliar with his MHMR history may have arrested him for false report to a police officer. Since he was sullen and gloomy, and I knew of his propensity to harm himself, I called his mother and she returned from work to safeguard her troubled son.

Typically, my average workday patrolling White Rock Lake on a bicycle yielded a few tickets, if that, since verbal warnings were also given for traffic and city ordinance violations. On one Thursday I had gone to court for a couple of hours, yet still had enough luck and time in my shift to return and arrest three people in separate incidents.

The first arrest took place on a pier where a few males were fishing. None of the men had a fishing license. I did a radio subject check and one of them had a couple of unpaid tickets from some years back. He went to jail. Oddly enough, he worked in a bait and tackle shop and knew that he needed a fishing license because he sold them all the time.

My second arrest occurred after I was stopped by a dogwalker asking for directions. I could see a female 50 yards distant was disconcerted by my presence and began walking back to her car at too frenzied of a pace. I broke contact and rode my bike to her vehicle just as she was about to leave and smelled freshly burned marijuana. I took down the names and DOBs of the driver and her passenger, then waited for cover to arrive. When I asked who owned the vehicle, the driver said the passenger, and the passenger said the driver. This aroused my suspicions that either the car was stolen, that something was in the car that they didn't want me to find, or both. My cover officers arrived, and I had the females step out of the car while I began my search for the marijuana or any contraband that presented itself. The driver informed me that there was a fake gun in the console. When queried she said the toy belonged to her 7-year-old cousin who was not in the vehicle. I didn't believe her; the realistic black 9mm toy pistol had been improvised with the magazine taped up to the bottom of the magazine well, making it longer and more menacing like a Tec-9. I didn't find any marijuana inside the vehicle. I arrested the driver for ticket warrants. After completing a short MIR (Miscellaneous Incident Report), I notified the Robbery section of the modified plastic pistol. I didn't buy into her story of it belonging to her cousin and thought it more likely that she or they may have robbed people.

The last arrest happened when I was riding back to the station to end my shift and stopped in a park parking lot ¼ mile away. There were three men and one woman standing at the bed of a pick-up truck still in their softball uniforms. I assumed correctly that they had been drinking alcohol, though only the woman still had beer in her bottle. Thinking it to be a quick alcohol in the park citation, I asked her for ID, but she didn't have it. Obtaining her alleged name and birthday but not having the benefit of a picture ID, I asked her how old she was. She hesitated far too long not being able to compute her age and cover her lie, and just said "Forty-something", with a smile. I told her that she was still 39, not 40, much less forty something. I called for a cover squad to access a computer, believing her to be lying to steer me away from her warrants. When we found her picture and name in a softball roster book, she relented and gave us her real name and DOB, which had ticket warrants. A co-worker still at the lake for one more hour was kind enough to take her to jail for me, where the flippant arrestee was charged with Alcohol in the park, her warrants, and Failure to ID as a Fugitive, this last charge giving her a criminal record.

I met with a security guard to retrieve some burglary tools that he had discovered as evidence from a burglary that had happed in the apartment complex the night before. While I was ending my conversation with him, I added myself to a call that was just dispatched involving a woman who had dropped her pants and squatted to urinate, as I was only one block away. Another security guard was standing with the woman adjacent to the puddled urine on the pavement. She freely admitted having urinated in public, though I couldn't write her a citation for it because I didn't actually witness the event. She stated that she had a weak abdominal muscle and tried to use a store restroom, but the merchant refused to let the woman use the non-public, employee only bathroom. She stepped outside onto the sidewalk between stores and emptied her kidneys. She was just given a criminal trespass warning by the shopping center security guard, and I documented it with a report. As I was finishing this call, another call was dispatched much further away, the details making it peculiar even for police officers. A woman was walking naked holding a pot-bellied pig and trying to shove its head into a neighbor flowerpot. I spoke to the assigned officer later about that call. He said that they had asked the woman in her 50's to just allow them to take her home and put some clothes on, but she refused so they admitted her into the Parkland Hospital Psychiatric Unit.

On any given day as a cop in a big city, you can have a vast array of calls.

I was working an off-duty job for a security company that provided security guards for what at the time in the spring of 1992 was a lively area of downtown Dallas called "West End Marketplace". They had several police officers every weekend working there to assist them. Minutes after I had signed in, I was asked to go with a couple of guards to the outside of a building because a man was being loudly profane while on the payphone and would often make derisive, derogatory remarks at people as they passed by walking. There had been several Aggravated Robberies in that area (common then), so when I arrived, I gave him a Terry Stop pat down for my safety. Other than squirm some he ignored me as he kept talking on the phone. I told him a few times politely to hang up the phone to talk with us, to tell his friend he would call him back, but I was consistently ignored. Before I ended his conversation for him by hanging up the pay phone, a security guard did it first. Now I had his undivided, hateful attention. One of the security guards asked him to leave the premises but our suspect said that he wasn't going anywhere. I told him that all he needed to do was leave, but he squarely looked me in the eyes and said he wasn't leaving, that we couldn't make him leave (wanna bet?). He said "Ya'll just hasslin' me 'cause I'm a nigga! Fuck you! Go Fuck yourself!" We moved in to grab his arms for the take down, but he pulled his arms in, and his body was near rigid as we took him to the ground and handcuffed him. Hoisting him to his feet, we escorted him to the security office, being denigrated and slandered by him every step of the way. There he was given the chance by the security supervisor that if he could just shut up and stop mouthing off for three minutes, that he would let him go. Being a stubborn nincompoop, our arrestee couldn't be silent and kept hurling unabated insults. He didn't want to stop running his mouth and I told him he couldn't control it, that all of this was unnecessary, but his bad attitude wouldn't let him cooperate. His version was that I had the attitude, and then thinking he could somehow give himself a modicum of control and self-respect, he told me to stop interrupting him when he was talking, and that I needed to shut up, adding that he didn't back down outside because he wasn't "a puss-ass nigga!" I told him that I was getting tired of hearing him talk and didn't want to argue with him. I also realized that he would calm down and be more tolerable if I walked twenty yards away from his unrelenting mouth and sat to wait for the on-duty-officers to transport him to jail for his criminal trespassing charge. As I walked away his comments to me were" Yeah, go on, leave you puss-ass! I'll remember you! I got your name. I got your badge number. You might get a slug in your chest!" He stayed relatively quiet after that. My having put distance between us calmed him down, but more importantly cooled me down before I became more agitated and did something I would regret.

A woman in her sixties hadn't been seen by her relatives for a while, and last spoke to one of her children five days earlier. Growing concerned, one of her sons drove over to her house.

After knocking and ringing the doorbell, he forced his way inside and found his mother lying dead in her bedroom.

I arrived and began walking toward the door when one of the teenaged granddaughters ran past me into the house crying. The son had covered his deceased mother with a white sheet to shield viewers from her progressing state of decomposition. I pulled back the sheet for a brief scan to determine that she had no obvious signs of a homicide. This woman was about 5'6" and 300 pounds and swollen from death. My speculation was that she had completed her bathroom trip and started to leave the bathroom. One of her bad knees failed her and she stumbled out the bathroom toward the bedside. Reaching out to brace her fall, she only slid the mattress over from one corner. Falling to the floor, she seemed to have struck her head on the metal bed frame. This either killed her, induced a fatal heart attack, or she fell because of a heart attack. Her postmortem lividity now caused a slow, constant seepage of a dark purple blood to ooze from her mouth which pooled around the bed frame and floor by her head. The Medical Examiner arrived and began to take pictures. The stench of decomposing flesh hung heavily in the stagnant air so somebody had the seemingly bright idea to open more windows and turn on the kitchen ceiling fan which was next to the bedroom of the deceased. This had the effect of stirring up the repulsive, abhorrent odor, and I gagged a couple of times. When the two men assisting the M.E. began to jostle the bloated body onto the reinforced gurney, the odor was too much for me to handle. Embarrassingly, I had to stifle some gags in front of the other officer and the deceased woman's son. I told them that I needed to get some air and went out the open back door then had to step away from the breeze coming from the doorway. They wheeled the deceased out wrapped in a colored plastic bag to minimize the sickening odor, then placed her into the rear of a station wagon for transport. I left pondering that if she had just used her metal walker that she had not brought into the bathroom with her that perhaps she may have prevented her death.

A woman flagged down an officer at White Rock Lake to report that her vehicle had been stolen. The officer sent out a BOLO message on the MDT computer. My partner and I decided to drive out to the nearby lake in the hope of spotting the stolen vehicle. Just a few blocks from where the vehicle was allegedly stolen, we spot it unoccupied in a parking lot, still at the lake. I checked the car for damage but there was none. No broken windows, doors still locked, her purse still on the front passenger floorboard (ladies, put those in your trunk PRIOR to visiting a park). I alerted the other officer by radio to bring his complainant to our location because her car was here undamaged, that she had forgotten where she parked. They arrived and the woman entered her car and checked her purse. As we expected, nothing was missing. She still insisted that she did not park her car there. The confused woman grumbled that no one else had a set of her car keys. She added that her nefarious boyfriend from 1 ½ years earlier had repeatedly played tricks on her trying to drive her bonkers (if so, he was succeeding). We were skeptics. Any chance of our believing her evaporated when she started rambling about some nonsense like ceiling paint that was bubbling with water dripping through, and that her ex-boyfriend had to be coming into her house because she saw unworn shoes pointing in the opposite direction that she had left them. When my partner and I heard those comments, we smirked at each other and abruptly excused ourselves and let the original officer handle the call.

A couple of dollar store employees watched a man put numerous items into his backpack and called police before he departed. I arrived and was told that he had gone next door to donate some plasma for money (never occurred to him to get paid first and then buy those items in the dollar store). Having a good description, I plucked him from about 30 people, returned the stolen property, and wrote him a theft citation.

A bank robbery call was dispatched and being less than a mile away I was the first officer to arrive on the scene. Bank officials had already separated the witnesses. I broadcasted a suspect description and the last known direction of travel in the red mustang in which the suspects had fled. Two of the witnesses were a young couple walking to the front door of the bank when the suspects bolted out the front door carrying a bag, jumped over some hedges, and entered the aforementioned vehicle. They correctly thought this action appeared suspicious, memorized the license plate, and were told when they entered the bank that it had just been robbed. Our helicopter and other officers participated in the search and located a different vehicle driven by the suspect, who was now wearing a different shirt. The bank bag with stolen cash was recovered within this secondary escape vehicle. The suspect was returned to the offense location where 3 of 4 witnesses positively identified him as the bank robber. Oddly, the teller whose window was visited by the robber found the experience so nerve-racking and was so shaken that she was unsure if he had been the suspect. She would be given another chance to possibly select him later from a six-photo lineup when her anxiety level dissipated.

It was New Year's Eve, 1994. I was working off duty security at the West End in downtown Dallas standing in an area known as

Dallas Alley with a colorful neon sign at the entrance. The cash register was ringing repeatedly from hundreds of patrons paying $20 to gain access to the four different bars inside. At about 10:15 p.m., with a human sea of hundreds waiting, admission was halted; a Fire Marshal had declared that the Fire code limit had already been exceeded. I had management make an announcement over a P.A. system that the Fire Marshal had closed access to prevent would-be customers from waiting any longer than they had to, so they still had time to leave well before midnight to go elsewhere. Many stayed in the outdoor plaza area but at least they would know that inside access had been disallowed until others left. Midnight arrived with a mini fireworks display from the outdoors plaza. All was peaceful and there had been no incidents requiring police intervention. An hour later that all changed. Given the enormous crowd of people inside and out drinking alcohol, some chaos and pandemonium were inevitable.

I was standing at the top of three steps when a woman yelled "Officer! There's a problem down here!" I saw over the crowd that there were three men shoving a guy into a corner. For some unknown reason I resorted to the full nelson wrestling move as I guided the closest suspect to another corner, telling him it's the police, and to cool it because it's over. Other officers and guards snatched the remaining two suspects and two of the three went to Detox. There were obviously many drunks at a New Years Eve party, but we only arrested the troublemakers. Forty-five minutes later I saw that a security guard was speaking to a couple, and I recognized the woman from an earlier loud argument. The guard told me that this time they needed to vacate the premises because they were inebriated. As I was walking over, I discerned that they were being asked to leave but were grumbling that they didn't want to leave. I told them that they needed to leave, or they would be arrested. The woman speechlessly dashed off into the crowded bar, followed by a security guard, her boyfriend, and then me. The security guard placed one hand around her upper arm in the escort position to guide her outside and maintain control. The boyfriend was aggravated over the guard placing hands on his woman, so he pushed the guard from behind. After weaving and bobbing through the crowd, I reached the boyfriend and placed him in an LVNR or a headlock. His legs went limp, and he lost balance, but so did I and we both tumbled to the floor. I rolled atop him, he rolled atop me and laughed, and I rolled back atop him taking him into custody with the assistance of an arriving officer. Two good Samaritans also assisted us with his drunken unruliness. While waiting in the office for the paddy wagon to arrive and transport him and his girlfriend to Detox, he complained of his eye hurting and blamed me for poking it. After the drunks were handed over and leaving, a security guard confessed to having pressed a thumb into the arrestee's eye to gain compliance. I advised him that could cause permanent damage and that in the future, he should try the pressure point notch behind an ear lobe.

I stopped a middle-aged man on traffic at White Rock Lake Park. He had no insurance but tried to brush off the violation by telling me that he didn't drive this car(?). I pointed out the obvious that he was driving the car, but he dismissed it by again saying he didn't really drive it anywhere, only in town for short distances and then not often. He had another car that he usually drove. I ordered a wrecker to tow his uninsured vehicle as required by our department policy, and explained to him that uninsured motorists like him are the reason why insured motorists must pay extra money on their policies for "Uninsured motorists". He wasn't listening to me and kept talking about how he didn't drive that car. Tired of his being naive and ignoring reason, I summoned a supervisor. I framed the situation, and the Sergeant told him that I had no choice and that I had to tow his vehicle. He continued his tiresome rant of not driving the vehicle. The Sergeant became quickly frustrated and knew that he would not listen and left. The wrecker arrived to tow the man's car, and then I offered him a ride home because it was starting to rain. He refused my offer twice and walked the couple miles to his home.

Days later I was called to Internal Affairs to answer to his complaint that I only stopped him because he was wearing a turban and that I was discriminating against Muslims, and that I forced him to walk home in the rain. I explained to the detective (known by some officers as "The Hammer") that the man was stopped for his expired registration which could easily be verified via a computer check. She was a thorough investigator and had already spoken to some of his neighbors to get feedback on the man's character. He was universally disliked and had no friends because he was rude and loathsome. He was known to say "Allahu Akbar!" out loud to scare some neighbors, then laugh at their frightened faces. He would also pluck up the small U.S. flags placed at the curb by the Homeowner's Association for some Federal holidays. Not one kind word was said about him by his neighbors. His complaint was dismissed.

On December 31st, 1999, I was working off duty for the Bank of America to protect their downtown building from the nearby revelers celebrating the city's first New Years Eve party, and from the unknown aftermath of the year 2000, labeled and feared by many as "Y2K". Many companies had spent many millions of dollars to upgrade their computers because there was widespread belief that globally, computers would fail to recognize a new century and millennia because they never had to before. This failure would totally disrupt commerce and there could be worldwide rioting and looting. When the clock struck midnight, there was a seamless worldwide computer change to the year 2000, not even a hiccup. There was a light New Year's Eve crowd downtown because of poor publicity, extreme cold, and year 2000 nervousness. This was the most regular pay money that I ever earned in my career. I was paid $50/hour for several hours, and then stayed an unexpected two more hours for $75/hour as a precaution for the potential year 2000 panic. I went home at 3 a.m.

A year, nine months and eleven days later from the above story was the worst terrorist attack in U.S. history. Three planes were hijacked by terrorists and slammed into and eventually collapsed America's tallest buildings, the World Trade Center in NYC, and destroyed part of the Pentagon. The fourth hijacked plane's destination was unknown as it crashed to the ground from a brave passenger uprising. Nearly 3000 thousand died that day on 09/11/2001. Americans went from feeling impervious to vulnerable in one day that shook the world. Most Americans at that time believed that more attacks would follow over the coming days, me included. One day later I was working my side job in the basement of Dallas' tallest building, the Bank of America. I'd be lying if I said I didn't think about another hijacked or stolen plane hitting the structure with me being a probable casualty. Though all commercial airports were closed for days, there were hundreds or thousands of small municipal airports with minimal security that were still vulnerable to plane thefts. My shift passed uneventfully.

I drove into a complex and saw a woman walking with some broken glass to put in the trash. I peered into a breezeway to find the apartment that had a domestic disturbance, and she asked if I was looking for Apt. 211. I was. She walked inside and I followed and saw a man who was her ex-boyfriend sitting on the couch. They had been arguing because she didn't want to give him a ride to work. She wanted him to leave, but he wanted to overplay his hand by staying until she offered him a ride. Since everything was calm and copacetic, I disregarded my cover officer on the radio. Within a minute, the argument started again, and he stood up from the couch and started to walk toward the woman. I interceded and guided him back to the couch, then asked the dispatcher to resume my cover. I let him use the landline phone so that he could call to have his mother pick him up, but when he and his ex- exchanged words again he jumped off the couch and heaved the phone in her direction. I stepped in front of him and with my hand to his chest forcefully backed him up to sit on the couch. I told him that he had been asked to leave and he needed to walk out, or I would arrest him for criminal trespassing. His reply was that he wasn't leaving, he had nowhere to go, that I would have to put him in jail. I told him that could be arranged. We had a stare down as I stood over him. He tried to quarrel again, but I told him to shut up and stay seated and my command went uncontested. The other officer arrived and the stubborn suspect who only had to walk away was jailed for Criminal Trespass.

On New Years Day 1995, I noticed a black Labrador wearing a collar with tags walking across the street dragging a leather leash. I pulled over and tried to get him to come to me to retrieve him for the owner, but after stopping briefly he skittishly moved away and walked inside a fence enclosure of a used car dealership. I closed the gate behind him to trap him among the dozens of used cars and called Animal Control. I didn't want him struck by a car, and the temperature was in the thirties. Another officer arrived and was convinced that we could catch the dog. I told him the dog was skittish and scared and would just run away and I wasn't going to run in circles trying to catch him. The other officer wanted to try, so we entered the fenced compound. The dog saw us and stood up, stood his ground, and growled at us with the hair on his back standing up. Abort! Abort! We decided to wait for the dogcatcher. When she arrived, she used a noosed pole to try to collar the dog, but he squeezed through a rear gate. I offered to mace the dog to incapacitate him long enough so that she could nab him, but she told us she would be fine and said she would capture him alone like she normally does. We departed, but several minutes later the dogcatcher had asked our dispatcher to have us return. I found that she had manipulated the dog back into the enclosed car compound. She was following the Lab along a fence. I approached with mace in hand, and we had the dog trapped. I was on one end standing in the gap between two adjacent cars, the dogcatcher on the other end, and the Lab caught in the middle. The dog moved quickly to sidestep me, and I shot a short mace mist at him. He yelped, and then squeezed out the front fence again where we had started. We tried to rescue him, but he was intent on escape, and I'd spent enough time on this call already. I cleared for another call.

An officer drove into a shopping center parking lot so that he could safely send some computer messages to another officer. Minutes later, the dispatcher reported that a theft was in progress at a drugstore just 100 yards away. He rushed over and stepped inside to find that the 35-year-old mother and 19-year-old daughter had gone behind the counter to steal cartons of cigarettes and were still dumping them into large white plastic garbage bags. He couldn't apprehend both, so the daughter escaped by fleeing on foot. I arrived to cover the officer and then orbited a bit to see if I couldn't spot the suspect at large. I could not and returned to be told that the teenaged store clerk had watched the suspects place stolen property inside their car still in the lot. I found that the thieving duo had already placed five white garbage bags of cigarette cartons in the back seat of their car, making the over $1500 theft a felony. Before we left for jail with the mother, her husband appeared and scolded her about stealing and because of her action we were towing their car. The daughter called 911 to report that she would be revisiting the store to surrender. We waited a while, but she didn't show so we left for jail after another officer arrived to wait for the daughter in case she had been delayed. While we were still at the county jail processing our prisoner, the daughter was brought in to join her.

Three teen males were seen in a neighborhood removing license plates from vehicles. Two officers had found the old brown and gray stolen vehicle in which they arrived. One of the suspects had left his wallet with a picture ID on the backseat. I added myself to the call and went to look at the picture before I began my search. He had dyed his hair a bright blonde, so this little villain would be easy to find if he was still outside walking. Witnesses were found that saw the kids attempting to remove a plate from another car. I had nearly ended my roaming search when I saw two teens crossing the street in front of my car only 20 yards away. I parked, exited, and called to them. They stopped. I knew that they were the right suspects because one of them had the dyed blonde hair from the picture that I had seen earlier. I grabbed each of them by their shirt collars and ordered them to get on the ground as I guided them there with a tug. One of the kids had a white t-shirt that I had unintentionally ripped nearly in half. As they lay on their bellies, one of my feet held down one of the suspects. I informed the officers that I had two of their suspects in my custody and gave my location. An off-duty Sergeant happened to be passing by and offered his quick assistance. I gratefully accepted. We handcuffed the two suspects, and the Sergeant followed me with them in my car to the location of the stolen car. Their fabricated story unfolded that some stranger in the stolen car asked them if they wanted a ride as they walked home from school (a special school for juvenile delinquents). They knew nothing about him but accepted a ride anyway. When he stopped, he just left and didn't tell them why he was leaving the car, then he just disappeared. One of the boys that I returned lived just one house away, but we had no witnesses that had seen the boy in the stolen vehicle. He was released to his mother. I drove the other boy home, trying to get information about the Phantom 3rd suspect/driver, telling him that I knew that he was lying and covering for someone. At his apartment, I told his older sister of the events, adding that her brother was stubborn and wouldn't give me the name of the driver in the stolen car. I added that I didn't care because his wallet was found on the back seat, and I would just charge him with stealing the vehicle. The sister burst out crying and shrieked to him that he needed to tell me what he knew. He relented and stated that his friend brought the car to school then offered him a ride home when the school day ended, and he gave me the name of this friend. I gave it to the officers that had initiated this call.

As a beat officer you will have to occasionally address complaints that citizens have about things happening on your beat. At White Rock Lake, bicyclists who used the streets all knew that by law the Texas traffic code stipulated that they must stop at stop signs, and there were a few signs there to remind them of this. The bicyclists on the road had the same privileges as motorists, but also the same obligations. Some stopped at stop signs, while others just put their head on a swivel and scanned for cops before they pedaled on through. I had to address a written citizen gripe about this very subject once. Enforcement action was expected to mollify any unhappy citizen. I was by chance behind three bicyclists on a block long road with an upcoming stop sign. They reached it and looked left and right to scan for police as there were no cars at the four-way stop intersection. They hardly slowed, only briefly not pedaling before they ran the stop sign. They never looked behind them. I followed and hit my air horn to pull them over. Visibly surprised, they did so. All were aware of the need to stop as required by law. Here with one contact, I could pacify my Sergeant and the complaint-generating citizen, but I opened my ticket book to find that I only had two tickets remaining for three violators. I voiced my dilemma and told them that I was only going to write two citations today, that one of them would receive a warning. They queried who would be the lucky one, and I told them that was for them to decide. One of them decided that their fate would be decided by a coin toss, with one of them saying "what could be fairer than that?" One of them made the coin toss, and I wrote my two tickets to the unlucky two and was on my way.

A week or more later, I received a computer message while in the field to report to Internal Affairs when I could. I sat down with an Investigator when I arrived to be told that two of the bicyclists had gone to Internal Affairs to lodge a formal written complaint that to settle who would receive the citations and who the warning, that it was my idea that they "gambled" with the flip of the coin. Fortunately, the other friend who had been riding with them--and who had actually received one of the citations--had been a man of honor and had already come in previously to refute the allegation of his friends, and his written version of events matched mine. I was cleared of any wrongdoing, and thankful for the man's integrity.

A man on a boat dock noticed another man in a small motorboat a distance out from shore. The second time he happened to glance that way, he was alarmed because there was no boat anywhere near where it should have been. Though he saw no one in the water floundering, he trusted his instinct and knew that the boat sank and called 911. The wind had picked up and there were choppy white-capped waves. A "Person in Danger" signal 44 was dispatched. I could see from our laptop screen that of the four officers at the lake, I was the furthest away, so I went to a sailing club to hopefully enlist the aid of their rescue boat. Through binoculars, another officer spotted what he believed to be a head bobbing in the water about 100 yards from shore. The Fire Department rescue boat started toward the unknown object in the water. I was close to departing in the sailing club rescue boat when I heard news on the handheld radio of another officer "The Fire Department is pulling a body onto their rescue boat now". I relayed the tragic drowning death of the other boater to several concerned sail boaters that were present; their hearts sank.

I drove to the other side of the lake and was surprised to find that the drowned boater was in fact just fine and was being examined by Paramedics before they released him. His shallow boat had capsized quickly from large waves. He grabbed his life jacket only to realize when he needed it that it was small, and he couldn't wear it. Rather than hold the life jacket to his chest and kick his way toward land, he decided to hold it between his knees and dog paddled with his arms. I advised the officer that had used the word "body" that better words like "boater" or "complainant" or "person" should've been used because anyone that heard the word "body" assumed the person to be deceased. I drove back to the other side of the lake to happily report the misunderstanding. They were relieved and appreciated my return to keep them in the loop. Semantics matter.

A man ran a red light. I stopped him and wrote a ticket. When he gave me an attitude, I gave him one back. Over the next 15 minutes our conversation evolved from there, and we are still friends to this day.

At night a young man still in his teens had unknowingly parked on one end of a cul-de-sac drive that had a hill in the middle at a park, thinking that he had parked in a parking lot. After stopping to talk with him I smelled weed and searched his vehicle when a cover officer arrived. I found no cannabis but did find it's smoke pipe, so he was the recipient of a drug paraphernalia citation. He also had an AR-15 rifle under his back seat. After checking the serial number and checking the man to confirm that he had no felony convictions which would make any firearm possession illegal, I sent him on his way. Texans, we love our guns.

Indian Casino Police in Oklahoma wanted an officer to visit an address to contact the mother of a 7-year-old girl who was found with an unrelated woman in their casino. Sheriff's deputies had brought the little girl to the Department of Human Services to hold until someone was contacted to retrieve her. It turned out that the girl had a 70-year-old father in an assisted living facility who suffered from Alzheimer's. The mother's caretaker informed the Sheriff's office in Oklahoma that the woman with the 7-year-old was her Kindergarten teacher but had permission to be her guardian. The problem arose when this woman received a criminal trespass warning to not return to the casino, but did so anyway, this time drunk and toting the little girl. She had been arrested for Criminal Trespassing, Public Intoxication, and Endangering a child. The little girl's life had so much turbulence and instability already, and now she had an aunt that started the two-hour drive north to become yet another guardian. But for how long?

A man was driving at a frenzied pace, weaving in and out of traffic lanes. A witness was very concerned at his recklessness and called 911 as he followed, convinced of an imminent accident. As the witness predicted, the fool who had a young child in the car T-boned another vehicle and forced it onto its side, then fled the accident scene. The crazy driver traveled another block, swerved into a shopping center, and sharply turned to park in a Starbuck's Handicapped parking space. He startled many coffee-drinking patrons who were sitting outside, including one who had a Concealed Handgun License and was carrying a pistol. He watched as the Hit and Run suspect hurriedly ran down a sidewalk carrying a Crown Royal bag. Seeing the terrified look on the running man's face, he asked him what he had in the bag. The suspect ignored him, so the curious java drinker followed from a safe distance. The suspect stopped and shoved the purple Crown Royal bag into a trash can, then rushed back to his car and sped away. The witness went to the bag that had been dumped, fished it out of the trash can and peeked inside. It was a gun and drugs, which he handed to a fireman when they arrived on the scene. I took possession of the bag and inventoried its contents before bringing it to the property room. There was a loaded .380 pistol, 21 baggies of cocaine, many baggies of marijuana, and numerous empty baggies. The paranoid suspect was found driving a few miles south and was stopped and arrested by two alert officers. I weighed, processed and deposited the drugs for the arresting officers who took the drug dealer to jail.

A small young man had gone to use a bank drive-thru and then departed. He noticed that a PU truck with three males seemed to be following him. To validate his suspicions, he changed lanes and took a couple of side streets. They continued to follow him. He parked in a yogurt shop parking space and surreptitiously called police to report the questionable but still present suspects who shrugged and denied knowing what our complainant was talking about. One suspect had a $5000 bond for Aggravated Assault warrant and was arrested. All the suspects lived hours away. I had the complainant leave first so the remaining suspects could not follow him again and did a suspicious person report that was forwarded to our Deployment Unit.

I was the "Courtesy Officer" at an apartment complex for over five years. In exchange for reduced rent, I had to respond to a pager that was activated by an answering service to respond to situations at the complex ranging from after business hours mundane lockouts and pool and clubhouse issues, to tenant complaints that might require an on-duty police response.

One such response occurred three times in four nights when a villain robbed three people at gunpoint. The complex was typically quiet, secure, and peaceful. In fact, the Dallas Police Chief himself lived there with his wife, as did another senior police official. One can imagine the panic and fear that overtook residents when they read the robbery crime bulletin that was left at each of their doorframe clips. I misled myself into believing that the perpetrator would not strike on Superbowl Sunday, and so felt somewhat comfortable about going to a friend's party to watch the game. The suspect was seemingly not a football fan as he robbed someone that day during my absence. Fearful residents started honking their horns if they arrived home after dusk in an audible attempt to dissuade the robbery suspect from choosing them as a target.

After the first Aggravated Robbery, I phoned the Police Chief's office to have him alerted to the potential lurking danger in our apartment complex. I also spoke to a Deployment Unit Sergeant within days to request surveillance from an empty third floor apartment which I had requisitioned from the management office, which gave them a clear view of the wall that the suspect used to climb into and out of the complex. I was stunned when he brushed me off even after I mentioned that the Chief himself lived here with his wife. He said they had a lot on their plate and wasn't sure when they could get around to it. I wasn't happy with that reply, feeling like he was shirking an important duty. Imagine the bad publicity from the department if no action was taken by the Deployment Unit and consequently the Chief and/or his wife were victimized at gunpoint. I spoke to the Watch (shift) Commander, and he saw things from my perspective, and I had a Deployment team doing surveillance from the vacant apartment in short order. Their second night there they observed the Aggravated Robbery suspect clamber over a wall and enter the complex, and he was arrested by them at gunpoint.

A day later I had the good fortune to deliver the news of our efficient police work to a concerned group of about 50 residents that attended a pre-scheduled Crime Watch meeting on the property, their unmistakable appreciation evidenced by their enthusiastic clapping and happy smiling faces.

A gunshot was heard from some people in a shopping center that was adjacent to a crime-ridden apartment complex. One woman had called the police to report having seen a male running with a pistol chasing after another male in a red car yelling "Get outta here Mother Fucker!" He was wearing a white tank top and khaki shorts, and a woman with uncombed hair was standing by an apartment armed with a shotgun. The witness showed us how she could see the quarrel through a pedestrian gap in the shopping center wall that led to the complex. My partner and I walked over and found three males sitting on a stairwell, one wearing a white tank top with khaki shorts. I had him step down toward me. I patted him down, then the others, but no one had a weapon. The teen that I patted down first had a week-old ankle monitor. There was an empty small blue drug baggie on a step near where two had been sitting, but they dismissed it by saying there were drug baggies all over the complex (no doubt there). Unfortunately, no one had warrants.

The next day I phoned the juvenile probation officer of the boy with the ankle monitor and told her of my incident. She phoned the boy's grandmother who lived in the same complex and was told that her grandson has been feuding with some other boys. I asked the probation officer to put a note in his file and keep track of his monitor signal in case of a violation. She was unaware of the distance needed to trigger an alarm on the monitoring device.

A bank was robbed at gunpoint by the same suspect that had robbed three businesses in our patrol division just the day before. We already knew that he drove a red SUV with tinted windows, and we had the license plate number as well. Shortly after the bank robbery was dispatched, my sergeant spotted a red SUV about a mile away on the same street as the bank which had been robbed. There were two discrepancies. The driver was a female, and the correct license plate of six digits was off by one. It was decided to be too much of coincidence. The woman could be a getaway driver with the robber laying low in the back, and maybe the license plate had been incorrectly reported the first time. Did the woman hear sirens of approaching patrol cars and panic leaving the bank robber to fend for himself? No, it was all just an uncanny coincidence. The real suspect vehicle was stopped several minutes later in south Dallas, though it was driven by a black male and not the white male suspect. The driver cooperated fully and informed us of the bank robber's home address. We surrounded the house and waited for SWAT. Earlier our Intelligence Unit had informed us that family members didn't want any harm to come to police and advised us that the suspect had said that he wouldn't be taken alive and would take some cops down with him.

Police made entry into his house, but he was absent, apparently having absconded prior to our arrival.

A woman in her 50's needed her car to go to work, but her car had been towed. She had reported her car as stolen but received a recorded message from a Detective informing her that her car had been towed because it had been repossessed. As far as the Detective knew, the case of her stolen car had been solved. But it hadn't. What the Detective didn't know was that the woman had owned her car for the past four months, paid in full to the previous owner. She even had a fresh title with her name and address typed on it that showed her to be the titleholder and lawful owner. She was distraught and sometimes crying as she explained the story to me. I phoned the owner of the car lot that had towed her car. I told him that the woman was the lawful owner who bought the car from another woman who apparently still owed a lot of money on the car but was never the full owner but sold it anyway without involving them. I told him that I didn't know how that had happened, but that he needed to collect the unpaid sum from the previous owner and release the car to the new owner who was an innocent party in this transaction. The car lot owner wasn't going to release the car until he received full payment from the original owner. I filed an at-large charge of Fraudulent

Transfer of a Motor Vehicle on the original female owner. I
warned the car lot owner to release the car, or I would charge
him with Auto Theft. I was told that I should do what I needed
to do. I phoned an Auto Theft Detective and explained the
situation, giving him my report number. I'm not sure how it was
finally resolved.

A married couple had been having trouble with their phone
reception. They had a phone repairman come to their house
and tell them that an unknown wire seemed to be causing the
crackling disturbance, appearing to have a direct feed onto the
phone line. This led him to speculate that it was an alarm
company connection.

Several weeks later an alarm company tech came out and told
the couple that he didn't recognize the wire; in his 13 years of
work, he'd never seen anything like it. This alarmed the couple.
The wife was a member of the Dallas School Board which at that
time was having issues with corruption, with some employees
running afoul of the law. A former Board member had some
unauthorized wiretapping of his phone and a voice tape
surfaced of him using a few racial slurs which led to his
termination. The school Superintendent herself resigned
because she tried to comingle taxpayer money to redecorate
her office. Her cover up had triggered a Federal Investigation,

ironic because she herself had begun to expose corruption and now she had become entwined in it. The couple feared that their line had been bugged, and worried that any off putting or unkind previous comment they had made on their private phoneline might be used for their downfall. The technician didn't think the unit he extracted looked sophisticated enough to be a listening device, what with a coiled center in a housing with two wires extending from each side. To err on the side of caution because the woman was an elected official, I contacted our Intelligence Unit, and they brought some debugging equipment. They also didn't recognize the unfamiliar unit. Their testing showed that the phone line had not been compromised by any listening device, but the unit still had to be identified as a precaution. A more experienced phone Tech came out and provided instant ID of the strange device. It was indeed taking intrusive priority over the phone line, but only to filter out interference from AM radio; it was an AM radio filter.

A man was using a three-foot-long board to shatter a couple of apartment windows. A couple rushed out of their bedroom to the front of their apartment and recognized the board swinging suspect as their next-door neighbor. Another witness saw the suspect earlier when he was walking toward her carrying the sturdy lumber and he told her to go back inside her apartment or her kids and dog were going to die. The woman scurried away, correctly thinking this guy had gone bonkers. I saw the suspect and ordered him to drop the board and put his hands on my hood. He launched himself so fast and so far onto my hood that his feet were off the ground. I searched and cuffed the suspect and returned him to the apartment complex where many witnesses identified him as the vandal. Though I didn't witness the incident, many witnesses did. I arrested him for a few ticket warrants and added the Criminal Mischief charge. At jail he saw a Jail Nurse for psychological reasons.

An 18-year-old man called police to report that he had just been robbed by four suspects. He told us the names of all the suspects because they were his friends. He had bragged to them that he had $580 on him (probably from selling drugs. At first, he told us he had saved the money then said his mother had given it to him. He was jobless). His purported friends decided that they wanted that money. As he walked away, one of the suspects called to him. As he turned to face them, one of the suspects displayed a pistol at his side and told him "You know what we want". The other three suspects latched on to him and rifled through his pockets, quickly finding his wadded cash. They thought that since the robbery victim was their friend that he wouldn't snitch on them by calling the police. They were wrong.

This was the second time that they had disrespected and wronged him. A couple of days earlier they had gone into his unlocked apartment where he lived with his mother and stepfather and had stolen most of his clothes. In fact, two of the suspects were wearing some of his clothes when they robbed him. The complainant told us that all of them had been known to carry guns, which apparently didn't bother him before until they made it personal. He had seen the suspects go to one of their girlfriend's apartments. Two officers went to that front door while I waited with my weapon at my side at the rear door. Having heard some whispering and mumbling by some people just inside the rear door. I radioed the dispatcher that we had heavily armed robbery suspects trapped inside an apartment and to send additional cover officers. About six more showed up having driven Code 3. Escape by the suspects now being impossible, we notified adjacent apartments of the potential for a gun battle and the residents vacated for their own security. I went to retrieve our complainant and told him to change clothes, then brought him to wait in a police car to identify the suspects when they stepped out or when we extricated them. When we were all in position—including one SWAT officer who happened to be nearby and now had his scoped rifle trained on the front door—we knocked. About 30 minutes had elapsed between door knocks, giving the suspects inside plenty of time to hide their weapons. A man and a woman came to look out the window, probably opining our level of preparedness. Finally, the door opened slowly and two of the robbery suspects cautiously walked out with their hands up. I had been using a wooden beam as cover and stepped out toward them ordering them at gunpoint to drop to the ground. They did so, and seeing the other officers handcuff them, I entered the apartment with three other officers. The girlfriend was just inside the door, and we directed her outside to awaiting officers, then bypassed her to locate the remaining two suspects but the apartment was empty. No pistols were found, only some ammunition. The robbery victim identified the two suspects now in our custody as having been two of the men who robbed him, and they were hauled to jail.

A man was at a grocery store customer service counter and attempted to buy some groceries with a temporary check. The employee discovered that the account had been closed and alerted the store manager. The manager informed the man that was trying to pass the closed account check of it being closed, and kept the DL that he had presented as picture ID. The shocked man realized his ploy hadn't worked and quickly turned and ran out of the front door, leaving the DL, a brown wallet, and social security cards behind, all of which belonged to another man. The manager pursued the man and obtained the license plate number of the getaway vehicle which he entered, and this getaway driver drove him from the location. A police officer spotted the car at the parking lot of the registered address. After waiting a short time, the getaway driver reoccupied the vehicle and then was quickly arrested. The first suspect was also arrested from an apartment within the same complex, and he had four folded checks from the closed account in his right rear pocket. An uncashed paycheck that was stolen from a mailbox was found inside the driver door panel. These two suspects which fit the reported physical and clothing descriptions were transported back to the offense location where they were positively identified by the store manager and customer service employee, and a customer who had seen both suspects, then taken to the County Jail.

While working at Sam's Club and standing by the exit door, I was approached by a man who began a conversation. Soon after, I noticed this man had "meth mouth", or rotting, decaying teeth and gums, accompanied by bad breath. I knew from observation that he had walked into the store with a male friend, and now suspected that this conversation was a diversion to prevent me from noticing the actions of his friend. Seconds later, his friend hurriedly walked beside me and out the exit door but wasn't carrying anything. I suspected that he had stolen CD's and DVDs, but had no proof, only that I had earlier seen him in that aisle. The meth head that had been conversing with me instantly broke off his conversation and joined his friend outside, and both were briskly walking away. I grabbed my radio and asked the dispatcher to send me some nearby officers to cover me on a couple of suspicious meth users that had just left the store and were believed to have stolen property. No one was available, and I wasn't going to confront them alone, especially now since they were off Sam's Club property. I broadcasted a description and direction of travel in case they become involved in a future incident.

On one Saturday night working downtown at a marketplace, I saw several Security Guards walking with a bare footed man up the stairwell that led to the Security office. His pant legs were rolled up and they were wet. It was upper 30's outside and raining. I asked about his lack of shoes, but the man told me that he had lost his keys and locked himself out of his car and needed to call his wife. I let him use a phone and eaves dropped. It didn't seem like he was solving his problem from what I heard. His conversation seemed disjointed and incoherent at times, but then I only heard half of the phone call. He hung up the phone then instantly demanded that he be taken to the airport. After I queried him about an alleged ride he had tried to arrange, he again said that he needed to go to the airport. I told him that I couldn't leave and said he should take a taxi. He had no money, and said he was expected in Washington tonight. Suspecting delusions of grandeur, I asked if it was state or D.C. It was D.C. of course. George Herbert Walker Bush was expecting him. I asked how he knew the President, and his reply was that it was his father. This was so long ago that I didn't know what President Bush's sons looked like because they had yet to rise to prominence, but I knew that one of them lived in Dallas. If true, he would've had Secret Service protection, but he was alone. I patted him down for weapons, then called 911 (no assigned radios at this time) to request two on-duty officers to transport him to Parkland Hospital under a Lunacy warrant. Barefoot, he had little awareness of reality and was a danger to himself, risking hypothermia in the cold and wet weather. My subject had no ID, so I tried to have him write down his name while we waited for his transport officers. I watched as he printed "John Fitzgerald Kennedy". I read aloud "So you're John Fitzgerald Kennedy?" Laughter erupted from the Security Guards in the office. Mr. Kennedy also laughed, but with a crazy maniacal laughter. He burst out laughing several times while he was detained, sometimes hysterically. Always, this was followed by a somber, melancholy mood when his eyes would water, and he was on the verge of tears. He was a neurotic, bi-polar manic-depressive who needed medication. He wrote down his birthday for me, which was probably correct. I asked him to write down his address. He took the pen in his hand and proceeded to write. Then he looked up at me and said, "My address?" "Yes! Your address. Where you live. Write it down." "Oh okay." He looked down at the paper, concentrated for a few moments, then looked up at me and predictably inquired "My address?" "Yes. Write down the street where you live." This time it appeared that I had made myself clear, as an "Ohhhhh!" look washed over his face. I thought finally, we were going to make some progress. He stopped writing and I retrieved the sheet and read it aloud "Russia 007". Laughter erupted again in the room, including from Mr. Kennedy. I ask him if he was living in Russia as a secret operative working for the CIA. Without hesitation, he elicited chuckles from the office by stating "No comment".

The officers arrived and I advised them of his mental instability and his need to go to the Psychiatric Ward. They had him stand up and searched him. He had only been a threat to himself thus far. One officer asked him to put his hands behind his back, and JFK asked "Why?" An officer told him that they were going to take him to get him some help at the hospital, and they were going to give him some shots. I thought why did he tell him that? Sure enough, JFK's arms became rigid and locked and he exclaimed that he hated needles. Each officer was now struggling to put his arms behind his back. Thinking fast and seeing a resolution, I said "Mr. Kennedy, they just want to escort you downstairs to speak with the reporters." Mr. Kennedy released the tension from his arms. Being relieved, he simply said "Oh, okay", and they left the office peacefully with JFK in cuffs.

A 27-year-old man met a 14-year-old girl. Shortly she revealed to him that she was a runaway from New York and had nowhere to go. The man had to have known that she was a juvenile because by definition, a "runaway" is a juvenile in every state. He had an ulterior motive and was far from scrupulous and sympathetic when he offered to allow her to stay a while at his apartment. Already knowing the difficulties and dangers of life on the streets, she accepted his invitation. Soon after in his apartment he told her that he wanted to have sex with her. The girl tried to give him the brush-off by saying "Not now, later". Unrelenting, he returned just an hour later. The underaged girl had just stepped out of the shower, having bathed for the first time in several days. She walked into a bedroom closet and closed the door behind her to have some privacy while she quickly put on some night clothes. Seconds later, the suspect opened the door and asked the girl if he could have sex with her. She replied no, and he urged her to change her mind before he got mad. The girl was only wearing a shirt and panties at this stage of dressing. The suspect pulled down her panties, stripped, then put on a condom. He guided her to the floor and then penetrated her. When he was nearly finished the rapist withdrew himself and ripped off his condom, ejaculating onto the girl's legs while he asked if she could feel it, did it feel good, and whose was it? The victim said his name and went to bathe again to use soap. We only showed up days later because a neighbor had reported a disturbance coming from this apartment. After hearing the girl's story, we arrested the man and took him to speak to a Child Exploitation Unit Detective, where he confessed to having sexual intercourse with the female minor who could not consent to sex with an adult because of her age. We took him to jail for Sexual Assault and several warrants.

A decrepit, shaggy, disheveled woman in her forties had been caught shoplifting and was being held in an office pending our arrival. I suspected the scrawny woman of being a drug addict, but carelessly permitted her to use the bathroom after her repeated requests before she was searched by a female officer who had yet to arrive. She finished rather quickly, and I pondered my error in judgment; she probably flushed any drugs on her person down the toilet. We took her to jail after the female officer found no drugs on her person after a search. I felt vindicated over my error when much to my relief during her search by a jailer, a small baggie of crack was found in her pants pocket. She had on two pair of long pants. The arrestee had forgotten to check her first layer pant pockets during her bathroom trip at the store. The weight of drugs she dumped earlier (if indeed she did) probably would not have made a difference, as it was still a felony. She insisted that it was just a piece of chalk, as if chalk comes in small cubes in tiny clear plastic Ziploc baggies. A drug test kit proved her wrong. The "chalk" was a "crack rock" and tested positive for cocaine.

Very seldom did I work behind the front desk, but when you did you performed some administrative functions, assisted walk-in citizens who came to the front window, and answered the phone. One morning, I took a call from a man with a whiny, scratchy, high-pitched voice who wanted to report that someone had thrown (Gasp!) a New York Times newspaper on his lawn! He had tried to call the Times to have them come pick it up (from New York?), but they wouldn't do it. Then he asked what I was going to do about it. I told him that I wasn't going to do anything, that if they didn't want their newspaper then he could read it himself. "I don't want to read no damn Yankee newspaper!" "Then throw it away". "I'm not going to throw it away! You're not from these parts, are you? Are you a Yankee?" "As a matter of fact, I'm from Chicago." "Ha! It figures. All of you damn Yankees stick together! Get me a southerner on the phone, I want to speak to him." "Sir, he's just going to tell you the same thing, just throw the newspaper away." "I will not! I want to speak to a Southerner!" Getting nowhere with this character, I told him to hold while I transferred him, but I hung up the phone on purpose. Seconds later, the phone rang again. Sensing that he redialed, I hesitated long enough so that someone else picked up the phone. It was our incorrigible, stubborn rebel again. After hearing an earful, the other clerk hung up and told me this guy occasionally calls for stupid reasons and wastes our time. Until he said that, I thought that someone was trying to play a joke on me.

I had just left a side job and was technically still on the clock because they allowed us to sign out at the closest quarter hour, so several minutes remained of my shift. Two blocks away I was the second car in a left turn lane waiting to get the green arrow. Seconds after I arrived, a tall lanky homeless man walked the crosswalk and stepped onto the median, stopping at the front left of my personal vehicle. I was sitting there in my police uniform as he unfolded a cardboard sign that read "HUNGRY. PLEASE HELP". Dallas has an anti-solicitation ordinance. I downed my window and told him to give me his sign. He said no. I instructed him that he was violating a city ordinance, and again asked for his sign. "Man, I'm not going to give you my sign, I need that!" I firmly stated to him to give me his sign. He apparently didn't know that he could be arrested or receive a citation for this infraction. He reluctantly gave me his sign and turned to walk back across the street but couldn't bite his lip and just had to shout out "Pussy Ass Mother Fucker!" My light was now green and I U-turned in front of him and pulled into the corner gas station where I stepped out. The homeless man now U-turned to avoid me and started to walk away. I called to him to come here. He replied that he wasn't coming there, how did he know that I was a real police officer in that car? I told him to look at my uniform and read the shoulder patch. I requested a one-man cover on my radio, then caught up with him and holding onto the scruff of his shirt collar guided him back to my car. The other officer arrived quickly, and we obtained the homeless man's identity. He had just arrived in town from Pennsylvania, and we found his ID on the police cruiser computer. I wrote him a ticket for violating the city solicitation ordinance, and then queried "Do you still think I'm not a police officer?" His attitude had changed, and he was quiet. I handed him his ticket copies along with a spiteful greeting of "Welcome to Dallas". He timidly walked away, now fully aware that the Dallas Police meant business, and he was far less likely to be disrespectful and discourteous to the next police officer who contacted him.

To deceive the cabbie, a 20-year-old man had him pick him up across the street from where he lived. The cabbie drove him 10 miles to a house that the 20-year-old visited for only 10 minutes. The cab driver returned him to a house that was purportedly his grandmother, but he never came out, so the cab driver called police about his uncollected $40 fare. The cabbie insisted that the man went inside the house, but the old woman inside was oblivious as to why he would say that because no one was there. We convinced her to let us search her house for her own safety, but we found no one. I brought a few picture frame photos of young men from her house to the cabbie outside in case this really was a grandmother protecting her grandson, but the cabbie said the man was not in the pictures. Another officer and I remembered a local miscreant that lived on the same street where the cabbie had picked him up, and that location was just a ½ block away. The cab driver showed us the spot where his fare started, and we recognized the duplex across from there as the residence of the young swindler. We mistakenly knocked on the wrong door of the duplex. Fortuitously, the man that answered was the father of the scammer, who told us his son lived behind the adjacent door.

Dad called his son and told him to come out and talk with the police. Junior didn't want to talk to us though and we caught him trying to slip out the side door without shoes. We handcuffed him for our safety and received a positive ID from the cab driver as the suspect in this "Theft of Service" call. The father paid his son's cab fare, satisfying the cab driver who went back to work. The 20-year-old son escaped the Theft of Service charge but went to jail for an outstanding Burglary warrant.

A maintenance man and an Assistant Manager observed two suspects enter an apartment using a crowbar and a hammer to remove the hinges from the rear door. I arrived and found that two of the three hinges had been replaced. My search of the apartment came up vacant. The TV was still on, and the burglary tools were inside a partly open drawer near the back door. The resident/complainant was reportedly at some unknown shelter and contact could not be made. Maintenance secured both doors which had been unlocked. I broadcasted a description of both suspects, with suspect 1 having an easily recognizable white and orange 23 jersey. Deployment was notified, and fifteen minutes later they spotted suspect 1 walking down an alley with two small children, then enter an apartment. I went to that door being watched by a Deployment officer. The suspect answered the door without his jersey and said that he had come from his mother's apartment with his young siblings. He was wearing an ankle monitor, so after my departure I tracked down and contacted his Probation Officer. She laughed when I told her that I had crossed paths with this probationer. She had just got off the phone with him. He was very angry with her because she was doing her job and warned him about leaving his apartment. He didn't like that. He had been argumentative, even speaking to her supervisor about being micro-managed. She had too much control over him, and he told her that he had stayed in the same complex just not in his apartment (as stipulated for his house arrest condition). Sooner than later, I think she issued a Probation Violation warrant for his arrest.

A man knocked on the door of his former girlfriend, but they had broken up three weeks earlier and she didn't want to see or speak to him. She had already started to date someone else. But her sweet two-year-old girl knew none of this and just heard someone knocking at the door, so she waddled over and opened it. The ex-boyfriend burst inside and started yelling "Where's he at? Where's he at?" The woman was near the door, and she could see that he was waving a .380 pistol. Fearing for their safety, she made a failed attempt to push him out the door, but he pushed her aside and rushed to the bedroom. Edgy and angry, not even waiting to see if anyone else was present, he entered the bedroom doorway and fired a bullet into the far wall. The woman took this opportunity to flee and ran outside and downstairs screaming in terror. He gave chase and caught up to her when she was almost at the top of a flight of stairs in the breezeway of another building. Grabbing her foot, he caused her to stumble. He crawled up beside her, held his pistol to her head and told her to give him a kiss and asked why she was doing this to him. They both stood up, and he tugged at her arm as he led her back to her apartment. At the base of the stairs, he probably accidentally fired a shot into the ground. This loud crackle startled her, and she scurried up the stairs and was able to enter her apartment and lock him out while he was in pursuit. She shouted that she was calling the police, and he left moments later.

When I arrived, several other women were waiting for me downstairs in the parking lot, all yelling and babbling at once. I singled one of them out and had her give me the suspect description and what she knew. We took a short drive in the neighborhood in the direction that the suspect was last seen running, but we didn't locate him. Upon my return the other officer had not yet arrived, and I went to the complainant apartment where I spoke with her and a witness. As I was there, the suspect called her on the phone. He wanted to apologize and come to see her. She found out that he was calling from a friend's apartment just two buildings away. I had to wait for the other officer to arrive. By the time that happened, the call had ended, and the suspect was no longer inside that apartment. He eluded us but would soon have an arrest warrant.

I had just stepped out of a Post Office inside a shopping center, having dropped some letters in the mailbox. As I returned to my squad car, I noticed three teen males that had just left an adjacent CVS Pharmacy. They had all been smiling and laughing, until they spotted me, fully aware of their truancy. I asked what school they attended and told them that I would be following them back to school. They pointed out their car and I had them hit the alarm key to prove that they weren't lying. Driving my police cruiser from a different row of cars, I noticed an empty spot where their car had been, surprised at how fast they had departed. I looked around and saw them pull out of the parking lot onto the street with no intent to wait for me. I rushed to close the distance between us, then told the dispatcher that I was following truants back to their school. I was a minute too soon. When I computer checked their license plate the vehicle showed to be stolen. Officers jumped on their radios to volunteer to cover me as I continued to follow the teens at or barely over the posted speed limit. They were zig zagging somewhat taking different streets but were generally traveling in the direction of their school. Meanwhile, I broadcasted our location to enable officers to find me. Our police helicopter arrived to cover me before other officers did. When enough of us were in place, I started the traffic stop by turning on my emergency lights, and others followed in sequence. By voice commands, the juveniles were extracted from the stolen vehicle one by one at gunpoint. The two passengers were checked and taken back to their school where officers completed a short FIR (Field Interrogation Report). I transported the arrested driver to the juvenile division to process him for Unauthorized Use of a Motor Vehicle.

Every dedicated Law Enforcement Officer doesn't stop enforcing the law just because he or she is off from work. It baffles me that people who witness a crime don't want to be a "snitch", so though they may live in and have a vested interest in the safety of their own community, they choose to ignore their civic duty. Their shirking of responsibility by not calling the police only allows crime to continue unabated and to worsen. If you see something, say something. You can remain anonymous. There is a myriad of ways that you can help the police and your community. Take action, get involved.

I was driving home from work and observed a male hastily running down a sidewalk. He had an unsteady gait and often looked back over his shoulder. It was plain to see that he was trying to rapidly evacuate from what I correctly assumed to be the scene of his misdeed. I called 911 to report this suspicious person, and soon discovered when she reviewed the calls holding with me that he was fleeing the scene of a nearby accident. Per a witness, he was believed to be drunk. I reported his location and the officer assigned to the call intercepted him.

Readers, if you see something suspicious, don't be dismissive of your gut instinct. Don't question your decision to call 911, you don't have to know all the facts. We beseech you to call and let us investigate and do our jobs.

Rolling through a grocery store parking lot, I could see a commotion up ahead and soon was being summoned by some people waving their arms. I stopped and entered the small crowd that had surrounded and were gawking at a man who was obviously having a seizure as he was writhing in contortions on the ground. I called for an ambulance. The humanity in us all compels us to want to do something. One person suggested trying to keep the man from clamping down and biting his tongue. I told him that we needed to not intervene because the man would only involuntarily bite a finger if one entered his mouth, and that an ambulance was coming. Another person tried to provide comfort by placing their hand on his shoulder. Not knowing whether the concerned onlooker intended to physically do anything more, the man having the seizure swatted her hand away knowing that his convulsions would soon pass. Another onlooker had some experience with a relative having seizures and commented that the seizure would be over before the ambulance arrived. I agreed, and by the time the paramedics were there, the seizure had ceased, and the man was regaining his composure. All we had done was keep him safe by forming a protective enclosure around him to keep him from trembling into the nearby parking lot while we awaited medical assistance.

As a bicycle officer at White Rock Lake, I noticed three vehicles whose drivers thought they were special. While everyone else had to park in the parking lot, these three guys found a missing short concrete post alongside the road. They drove between two of the short posts across the grass and parked under some shade trees. I would always use the analogy with these people that if they had visitors at their house, would they park on the street, or on their front yard? The City of Dallas was no different. It's a good reason for contact to check for warrants too.

I approached all three males and requested their ID's. While talking to them, a two-year-old boy with them toddled over and started touching my bicycle which was supported by the kickstand. Within seconds, he was pushing my bike, and it began to topple over. Nothing was said by the toddler's father. I reached out to prevent my bike from falling to the ground and said I can't let you do that buddy and gently guided him away by lightly holding an arm. As he stopped where I wanted him to be, his unsteady balance caused him to fall backward onto his keister and he began to cry. This upset the father who now accused me of pushing his son to the ground. They saw what had happened, but I explained it anyway, and asked him "What was I supposed to do, let your kid push my bike over? I didn't hear you say anything". I could see the ire on this man's face. I checked all three subjects by radio, but the only one with warrants was the disgusted father who glared at me angrily. I had backed away a bit to do my subject checks but was still within earshot of the father when I heard him say softly to his two friends "Let's jump him man!" They were visibly shaken and had widened eyes at the suggestion and knew that I probably had heard that comment. He again said "Let's jump him! C'mon man, lets jump him!" but his friends would not be incited to assault an officer. They had no warrants, so cooperation was natural. I slowly put distance between me and the group and told the dispatcher to start me some cover, adding "Code 1 for now". This request for cover at normal speeds "for now" got me a few volunteers to start my way. Of course, after they arrived I had no more threatening comments from him. I arrested him for his ticket warrants. One of his friends called the arrestee's wife to come to the location to retrieve their son. She arrived and introduced herself to me as an attorney, asking me politely what my "PC" (Probable Cause) for contact had been. I told her, and she had no further comment.

On the way to jail and at the jail, this arrestee kept talking smack, telling me that I feared him and that's why he wore handcuffs, that I only had power from my badge. At the jail as he was being processed during book-in, he told me that he should just kick my ass. I told him that we were being recorded. If he thought a trip to the hospital and then to prison would be worth it, then go for it. It resonated with him. He smartly reconsidered given the minor misdemeanor charge that he had from his unpaid ticket warrants. We continued showing our contempt for each other by having a stare down that lasted until the jailers finished processing him and I exited the door.

I had a traffic stop and had the driver get out of his vehicle for some sobriety tests. He had some issues that made it more difficult to determine if he was intoxicated. He was a Vietnam veteran and walked with a limp, he wore glasses, and he'd had a tracheotomy. I smelled alcohol on his breath, and he had HGN (Horizontal Gaze Nystagmus, an involuntary bouncing or jerking of the pupils as a symptom of excessive alcohol or drug consumption). Oddly, he also had steady balance and spoke clearly without any slurred speech. If he was brought to jail and found to not be drunk, I might have to release him and take him to get his car which I would have had towed or take him home. He might be a waste of my time, and his arrest might be a waste of his time and money. I decided that I would risk it, and arrested him for DWI, believing him to be legally drunk enough for a DWI arrest prosecution. His breathalyzer result of .33 at the jail showed him to be drunk alright; he was 4x the legal limit. I had to take him to the hospital to have him treated for possible alcohol poisoning from having over-imbibed.

An older woman was watching TV in her bedroom @10 a.m. when she heard a loud noise. She didn't think much of it, like perhaps the wind had blown something over outside. She walked to the front door and saw that it was open and saw a board from the inside door frame lying on the floor. It didn't register with her what had happened. She closed the door, then turned around and screamed when she saw a tall skinny man facing her in the hallway just ten yards away. She ran through the kitchen area with the would-be-burglar following her saying "Don't move! You better stay here! Come here or I'll kill you!" After running around inside her house, she slipped out a side door and scrambled to a neighbor's house where she called the police.

The suspect was gone before I arrived. The woman moved out quickly, being gone in less than a week.

A public bus pulled off to the right shoulder and unloaded a male passenger. This man for some unknown reason was in such a hurry to cross that he rushed in front of the bus, but the driver noticed and quickly braked to allow him to pass. The pedestrian ran across traffic lanes, somehow avoiding being struck by an oncoming vehicle. He narrowly escaped death when he continued to cross the middle lane. As he galloped into the left lane, a woman driving the speed limit of 40mph slammed into him with a direct hit. The man landed on her hood, struck her windshield, then was airborne backwards over her car. Some witnesses from inside the bus said that his lifeless body looked like a rag doll as his limbs flailed when he was flying in the air. He was dead because he couldn't look both ways before he crossed the street.

After I saw a man run a red light, I stopped him and found him to have some ticket warrants. The traffic stop of this church van was on the church parking lot. While some of his students watched from a distance, I arrested their youth minister. It probably became a life lesson for them about personal responsibility or the dangers of procrastination.

There was a verbal domestic disturbance at a house with no criminal offense having been committed. We asked if either the husband or wife could spend the night at the house of a friend or relative to assure a night of peace, but both were pigheaded and neither wanted to leave. We arrested them both for their ticket warrants and took them to jail.

I was a "Courtesy Officer" who lived at a reduced rent in exchange for responding to minor issues after hours within the apartment complex. I tried to not involve on-duty police if I could handle problems myself, but sometimes for my safety I had no choice. I went to an apartment after receiving word from the answering service about a tenant having called about a loud disturbance in another apartment. I went there to listen from the breezeway and heard objects being broken, grunts and groans, and shouts from the people inside. I phoned 911 and waited for the police to arrive. When they did, they banged on the door and announced, "Dallas Police!", and all of the commotion suddenly stopped. The silence ended with a male opening the door. We reported to him and the two other young men in the apartment that they had been making a lot of noise and asked what they had been doing. No one was hurt, and their story matched the evidence. They had been drinking and decided to destroy pieces of furniture with a hammer and a small axe, and some other hand-held tools. That wasn't illegal, but it was entirely too late, and they were disturbing their neighbors and agreed to stop their destructive fun.

They were former college roommates who had a reunion: a doctor, dentist, and a lawyer.

I was taking a drink break at a 7-Eleven and was ready to leave. The clerk friend of mine asked me to stay a bit longer because it appeared to him that two men outside were stalling at the gas pump and waiting for me to leave so that they could drive off without paying. His instinct was correct. They were looking toward the front door, and finally decided to come inside to explain their situation. They had pumped $12 of gasoline, but only had a fraction of that money for payment. The clerk informed them that they needed to somehow come up with the remainder. They looked under their seat, asked a couple of customers at the pump, but still came up short. I asked for a one-man cover, then went out and obtained their IDs for a computer check. Both brothers were wanted, one with a Parole Violation, the other with a Probation Violation. They were arrested after the other officer arrived, and their car was towed.

A family had just moved into an apartment from Louisiana. They were unaware that their new complex was full of ne'er-do-wells. They unloaded all their furniture, but just a few days later, granny became homesick and insisted on being brought back home. Everyone loaded up and brought their suitcases, telegraphing to observers that they were going to be gone on a trip for a while. Probably not too long after they left, some of their neighbors decided to make themselves at home in their new home and kicked in the door. Unhurried, they relaxed and came and went, as did their friends too, I'm sure. They became so indifferent about their trespassing that they cooked food from the new family's refrigerator, using the new family cookware. When the new family returned without grandma two weeks later, they had a completely empty apartment. Nothing was left behind except a dirty stove, and the body odor stench of many people having been in their apartment. No neighbors were kind enough to tell them who had been inside during the previous two weeks.

I once had to lecture a couple of young kids because their own nearby parents simply didn't care enough to say anything. The young grade school aged brother and sister each had a pile of rocks that they were throwing at each other from a distance with a row of cars about five yards away from them.

I became engaged in a heated discussion with a young man debating a topic which I cannot remember. After five minutes, it ended, and my partner asked why I didn't arrest him for Disorderly Conduct. In truth, I had a charge and a thrill from the verbal sparring. The next week, the same young man approached me and extended his hand. As I shook it, I was surprised at his reconciliation and asked him why he was doing it. Respectfully, he simply said "We cool man, we cool."

I had just started my shift and was driving at White Rock Lake. An Auto Theft detective had our helicopter following a suspicious vehicle from a storage rental business. The suspects had just parked a stolen truck there (later found to contain 60k of stolen property) and were now in a car leaving the location. The suspects knew that the helicopter was flying overhead and correctly surmised that they were being followed and increased their speed. This was at shift change time, and no officers were available. As the car neared, I volunteered to assist "Air One", as did an off-duty officer driving a police car working neighborhood patrol before his regular shift started. We both started to the area where the three suspects were driving. Knowing that they could not outdrive the police helicopter, and not wanting police cars to arrive, the suspects abandoned their car and ran off in different directions. I had just entered the neighborhood and the chopper directed me by my cruiser number on the trunk of my car to turn right down an alley, which I did. There far ahead of me I could see one of the suspects running. As I gained distance, the suspect cut right to go between two houses out toward the next street. I could not follow so continued to the alley end, turned right, and right again onto the same street. There I observed the suspect walking down the sidewalk, trying to blend into the neighborhood like he just happened to be there for a stroll. I was wise to his trying to hide in plain sight and stopped 10 yards behind him. I stepped out and ordered him to the ground at gunpoint. He complied and dropped to his knees. When I reached him, I pushed his back to force him to the ground and cuffed him. Despite originally being undermanned, within three more minutes others had the other two suspects in custody. My arrestee was only 24 years old with a wife and two children, aged 3 and 4. He had conversed with me as I took him to the Auto Theft Unit to provide a statement. For the sake of his family, I had hoped that he took my advice and continued to be cooperative.

At near 1 p.m., I was searching from my vehicle for a stolen car suspect who had ditched the vehicle and was now running from police, but his exact location was unknown. As I turned the corner into a nearby intersection, I observed a man wildly waving his left arm to get my attention. I had to U-turn, and I looked in my rear-view mirror and saw a man running. I assumed that it was the suspect that I had been looking for and broadcast a description of him for other officers involved in the search. An anonymous citizen informed me that the suspect who had run was now behind the Burger King, and I directed officers to that location. He was soon in custody. He was not the suspect that we had been searching for, however. The man that flagged me down told me that this suspect was involved in a Hit

& Run further up the street. I asked the dispatcher from that different patrol division if she was holding any calls involving the vehicle from which the captured suspect had fled. She had a related UUMV (stolen vehicle) report that had not yet been assigned. I had her give that to me to do later at the jail since I had that thief in custody. Another officer had been assigned the Hit & Run, so I gave him my report numbers and arrestee information. I looked up the stolen vehicle offense report and phoned the owner so he could retrieve his vehicle and avoid having to pay a towing and City Auto pound storage fee. The car keys were in the ignition. I waited a short while, and the owner arrived. He asked who had been driving it, and I told him that we had the suspect in custody in the backseat of a nearby police cruiser as I pointed at it. He took a gander at him and said "No, no, no, no. It can't be!" as he walked over there with me shadowing him. He continued, "I can't believe this! This guy is one of my son's best friends!" and told the prisoner through the glass "You've been in my house a hundred times!" The arrestee had his head hung low and didn't say a word.

We never did find the original car thief. His lucky escape probably only happened because all the officers that had been looking for him were redirected by me to look for what became another car thief.

A bar manager noticed an inventory shortage of his beer and liquor. Trusting his gut instinct, he had faith in his bartenders and employees and suspected the morning cleaning crew of stealing the booze. He devised a plan and arrived early one morning and parked his car off to one side to have a view of the rear door. The cleanup staff arrived and performed their tasks. As they prepared to leave, one curious male walked over to the lone vehicle in the parking lot, but all he saw was a man (manager) presumed to be asleep with some empty beer bottles around him. Satisfied that this was just some drunkard, the cleaning crew began their usual routine of loading up "free" alcohol into their car. The manager called 911 to report the Theft-in-Progress. I was close and arrived quickly...too quickly. The thieves had only loaded one case of beer into their trunk before I arrived. This was only a M/C amount, so I could only write them each a Theft citation. They were given a Criminal Trespass Warning by the manager and lost their jobs after the manager called to report them and cancel the cleaning company service.

During the day on New Year's Day 1995, another officer and I made two separate trips to the county jail with a prisoner. Both men had been drinking heavily and had assaulted a loved one. On each of these trips, we were the only officers at the county jail processing a prisoner (rare). There can't be too many worse ways of starting off a new year than by being handcuffed and placed in jail.

It was Halloween night, and I could see up ahead on the road at White Rock Lake that a somewhat large group of young, costumed kids were running down a yard in an attempt to scare motorists that passed by on the parallel 25mph road. Their scare scramble was accompanied by their attempt at deep scary monster groans. All they could see on each vehicle as it approached were the two headlights. Less than a hundred yards away, I was next in line. Initially, I received the same exact treatment. After a few seconds though, their lame deep monster voices of "Ahhhhhhhh!" became a much higher pitched "Ahhhhhhhh!" as they ran away screaming "It's the cops! It's the cops!" Their Halloween fright night became a frightened night.

A woman was living with her 13-year-old son in her boyfriend's apartment. When she went to bed, her boyfriend was getting drunk. She awakened with her boyfriend's hands squeezing her throat with him in a rage loudly declaring that he was going to kill her and her son. Her son was soon in the bedroom to intervene and protect his mom as he punched the attacker on his back and the back of his head. The drunken boyfriend angrily tried to attack the son but couldn't catch him as he ran outside the apartment. The woman saw her chance and locked the front door behind the battering boyfriend as he departed. The man cannot get back into the apartment, so he retrieved a shotgun from his truck and used the butt of it to bash out his own apartment windows, accidentally brushing up against glass shards still affixed in the windows and lacerating the right side of his head. The woman fled out the rear door and called police.

I arrived and saw a large crowd of bystanders in a courtyard area on ground level with several of them assisting me by pointing up into the darkness. Someone else had phoned the police to report the disturbance prior to the battered woman doing so, and I could still hear glass breakage from somewhere up above me. I started to run up the stairs after I observed a shadowy figure make a dash up on the second level. I heard something metallic strike the concrete ground down below near the crowd. Unseen by me, the drunk male had been warned that the police were present and had thrown his loaded shotgun to the breezeway sidewalk below him. I couldn't see anyone on the second floor because of the darkness anyway, so I went down to confiscate the 12-gauge shotgun. After trying to obtain some witness information, we were told by the manager that our suspect was observing us and trying to be inconspicuous by hiding in the crowd. We took him into custody, and I unloaded the single shell from the shotgun chamber. We went to Parkland Hospital first to stitch up the arrestee's head wound from the broken glass, then on to the county jail.

A neighbor phoned police because a young married couple was having a petty argument over car keys, and who got to drive their only vehicle. The neighbor wondered how they could still be together because they argued all the time, and he thought this dispute could lead to physical violence like some others.

Neither of them had a DL, only ID cards. I checked them both on the computer and they had warrants totaling near $3000. They both went to jail.

I heard from another officer that though they were each only 20 years old, they were so irresponsible that they already had their two young children removed from their home by CPS.

A girl at a grade school reported to her teacher that the previous Friday night, she and a friend had seen a woman throw a baby into a dumpster at about 9 pm in the Fair Park area of Dallas. The teacher notified the school Principal and called police. I arrived to find out from the girl that she was a runaway, but she still decided to go to school. She said that she took two public buses to get to her friend's apartment complex the previous Friday, but she didn't remember the complex name or the street name, only knowing it by sight. As they sat on the front steps of her friend's apartment, they observed a woman in the distance with a jacket over her extended arms walk over and place something in the green dumpster. After the woman walked away, the curious girl and her 14-year-old friend (who reportedly would never talk to police) walked over to peer inside. There they could clearly see from a nearby light the body of a naked, dirty, dead female baby atop some trash in a corner of the dumpster. When I asked what was near the dumpster, she stated that there was a blue two-story house with a porch that was next to the small complex, and that there was a one building apartment complex on the opposite end of the complex. She said that sometimes she and her friend went through a hole in a chain link fence to walk across a narrow grassy area with some trees to get to the back of a KFC restaurant. Not knowing when the trash might be emptied, I had the girl draw me a map, then gave it to another unit when they offered to drive the girl and her mother around that area, as it was better known to them. Once in the area, the girl said that maybe it was a Church's Fried Chicken restaurant. Minutes later she admitted to them that she never saw a dead baby in a dumpster, she had only heard about it but didn't know where or when it had happened. The officers drove the girl and her mother home, frustrated over having wasted their time and concern believing the girl's fallacy and imagination, as I was. I had to call back my supervisor, the Homicide Unit, and Child Exploitation to tell them that this deceased infant call was just an absurd farce. Upon completion of my report, I had wasted three hours. The next day, I returned to the school with another officer. We had the principal pull the lying student from her classroom, and I arrested her for False Report to a Police Officer.

I was one of four officers standing at the corner of a building talking to a suspect from our call. A large young man not connected to this situation decided that rather than walk around us (plenty of room), he would walk through us, and brushed up against some of us as he did, not saying a word. His size was the source of his courage, or foolishness. Our focus now shifted to him having tried to intimidate us. After we obtained his ID, I saw that he had just one outstanding ticket warrant from Dallas PD. Normally, that would just require another citation, but I decided that he needed to be arrested for it given his brazen, reckless intrusion, and took him to jail.

I had two vehicles that had been burglarized in a small hilltop parking lot overlooking White Rock Lake on the north side. One of the car owners was a young college girl who had gone for a jog and returned to find her car window broken, and an expensive purse that her dad had given her for her birthday had been stolen. She was distraught over it because of its' sentimental value and cried. While taking the reports, a jogger returned and saw what had happened. He informed me that it may not be anything, but as he was stretching to leave that same parking lot to begin his run, he noticed two males and two females in a vehicle with an Illinois license plate. They parked and re-parked a few times, pulling forward and backwards before they settled on a space. I made a mental note of it and returned the very next day at about the same time. There was the same vehicle, backed into a parking space with four people in it observing their surroundings. I asked the dispatcher for cover on the suspicious vehicle and made contact with them getting their ID's. Cover officers arrived and I framed the situation for them. After speaking to the driver, he agreed to allow his vehicle to be searched, and he signed a Vehicle Consent to Search Form. In the trunk, I found several items of property that I believed had been stolen, including the 19-year-old girl's purse from the night before. I confiscated the property to place it in our property room as Found Property, and linked the previous night's report numbers, listing those four occupants as the suspects. We could not arrest them because no one had seen them in the commission of the burglary acts. I had the pleasure of calling the young college girl to report that I had recovered her purse just one day after it was stolen. She couldn't believe it, and cried tears of joy over the phone as she thanked me.

A couple weeks later, she sent me a Thank You card praising me as her hero with a $10 Starbucks coffee gift card enclosed.

Three gang members of the "Crips" street gang were casually walking down a sidewalk inside an apartment complex one night. A Ford Probe sports car approached them from behind and suddenly fired several shots from the vehicle at the three pedestrian Crips. The Crips began to run. One was struck in the arm as he rotated to run and left a whisked spotted trail of blood on the wooden fence behind him. Another was struck in the stomach and hand. The third was unscathed. All three ran through a breezeway to escape death. Two of the four rival gang member "Bloods" jumped out of the pursuing vehicle in this drive-by shooting to chase down the running Crips. The two armed Bloods gang members stepped into the breezeway entrance and discharged several more rounds in the direction of the fleeing Crips. The loud echo of the gunshots led some witnesses to believe that a shotgun had been fired, but they were in fact handguns (we found the spent shell casings).

This was a warm summer evening, and many apartment residents had been outside when the shooting began and naturally ran for safety. They mistakenly believed that when the two shooters got back into their vehicle, that the violence had ended. They began to emerge out of curiosity. Much to their fright, the Blood suspects had only circled the block and returned for more gunplay, shooting at anyone that they saw hiding hoping to hit one of the rival Crip gang members. They did this one more time, but then heard police sirens and sped away and fled the scene. Somehow no additional people had been shot during their two additional forays.

The gang members who had been shot were in stable condition at a hospital but refused to finger any of their assailants that had pulled the trigger.

Years later, to the joy and relief of police and homeowners in the area, this seedy apartment complex and a couple of adjacent complexes were condemned and razed to the ground to make room for a new High School.

A woman told me that a man that she knew was wanted for Escape. I checked his provided name and DOB and confirmed that he had that outstanding warrant. The helpful and probably vengeful woman gave me the address in a different patrol division in Dallas where she knew the suspect to be hiding. I switched to that radio channel's dispatcher and informed her and other officers on that channel of the street name where a known fugitive with an active Escape warrant was believed to be holed up, and asked if anyone was interested to go to Channel 10 (our go to alternate channel if too much needed to be said to keep open the primary channel). Several officers gave their Unit numbers to inform me that they were listening on CH10. I gave the suspect details and address, and asked if they could meet each other somewhere nearby that address, and then coordinate their arrival as a group with known positions around the house to minimize the suspect's reaction time.

After the operation, one of the officers contacted me. The suspect was found to be at the house, was taken into police custody and was on his way to jail.

I was due to end my shift in 15 minutes but thought that I could take a quick call from among the still holding unassigned calls. I found an alarm call near my police station. I had the dispatcher assign it to me without any cover because 98% of Alarm calls are false.

 I arrived at the house to find the front door closed but unlocked without any indication of forced entry. The alarm was no longer audible. I didn't inform the dispatcher of my having an open door because she was busy and I was just going to do a quick visual and physical sweep of the house, then lock the door behind me. I pushed the door open with weapon drawn to begin my search. As I was slowly moving down the hallway, the ear-splitting high decibel alarm began sounding again with such intensity and suddenness that it startled me. But it apparently scared this little dog much more as he came running out of a bedroom and directly toward me. His tail wasn't wagging, and he continued running toward me until at the last second, he darted between me and the wall. I spun around to see him run out the front door which I had left open. Crap! I chased after him as he ran across the front yard, and continued after him as we crossed a side street. The little pooch was observant and when I slowed down, he slowed down. When I ran faster, he ran faster. I finally amped up my horsepower and was ahead of the dog. The dog turned and scampered back to the house. He ran into the back yard, which is where I should have left him. I found him at the back door and had it in my mind that I was going to scoop him up and put him back inside the house. Poochie had other ideas. He scooted around me and ran to the front door of the house, but I had closed the door behind me when I left to pursue him. Now he ran to the back again and I watched him scurry behind a woodpile. I went to look and saw a steep riverbank behind that pile with a river down below. I didn't see any ripples, but did he fall in? I hoped that he had wiggled under a hole in the neighbor's fence, but I thought he might be floating down that river. I told the neighbors, who calmly told me that the dog was territorial and was probably just fine somewhere. Still not reassured, I went back inside the house to leave a note apologizing for their dog having run off and locked the door behind me.

As I was leaving, I saw the dog reappear at the back yard entrance looking at me excitedly with his tail wagging, like he thought that I was playing with him and wanted me to chase him again.

I was driving slowly through a motel parking lot checking license plates on my computer in the hopes of finding a stolen vehicle. I found one, a 1999 Jeep Wrangler. Knowing that vehicle info is requested at check-in, I went to the office to determine if the owner was checked into the motel or if it perhaps belonged to a visitor. I was told that the driver checked out the day before, so I ordered a wrecker and began my wait. The motel clerk stepped out to speak to me minutes later and apologized, saying that he had made a mistake and that the driver of the vehicle had not checked out and was in Room 120. I came up with a plan on the fly for the clerk to go to the suspect motel room and inform him that the sprinklers were about to come on and ask him to move his vehicle to prevent it from getting wet inside. As he walked over to do this, I positioned myself nearby so I could observe the Jeep Wrangler get occupied. Minutes later, I saw a male with keys in his hand enter the vehicle, and he backed up to re-park it several spaces down. As he did this, I swooped in and turned on my emergency lights. He was blocked in between my vehicle, other cars, and the building. I rushed out to overwhelm him at gunpoint and he surrendered and was cuffed. The vehicle was confirmed stolen, towed to the auto pound, and the arrestee went to jail for the stolen car and some State Trooper warrants.

An intoxicated woman was walking near an apartment complex office and decided to pull open the passenger door of a vehicle. She sat down as the owner was seated in the car. He told her to get out, having no idea who she was. She ignored him, and removed her bra from under her shirt and placed it on the seat between them. The man stepped out of his car and went into the office to phone police.

We arrived and quickly found her to be a vociferous, derisive, name-calling jerk. This foreshadowed what was to come. Neither of us could smell alcohol, so to give the woman the benefit of any doubt, we called an ambulance to check on her blood sugar as she declared herself to be a diabetic. Her blood sugar was normal, so she was simply drunk, and we cuffed her for a trip to the county jail. Besides her drunkenness, she only had one ticket warrant but with her having diabetes we had to take her to jail to see a nurse and could not just take her to Detox. She became my immediate tormenter, several times calling me a "Mother-fucking white man!" which sounded bizarre coming from a white woman. When we arrived at the jail sally port, she suddenly had a change of heart and flipped to trying to be nice and friendly, saying that she was sorry, and asked if we could please just let her go. Not getting the cooperation that she desired from her play-acting, she switched back to being vitriolic. I had shaved my head just a few days before to make my growing male pattern baldness invisible. Never holding back on what she was thinking, she started calling me "Baldy". Not having come to grips yet with my baldness which caused me to shave my head, being tagged as "Baldy" got under my skin and irked me. As the other officer was filling out the standard jail Book-In form, I told him to write "Nose wart" under the scars, marks, and tattoos section. My retaliatory comment had the desired effect of striking her nerve, and she angrily spewed out that I was ignorant, that it was actually a beauty spot (it was a wart).

A teenage boy was seen by store personnel concealing $10 of products in the front of his pants and was detained as he tried to leave. Asked if he had ID, the teenager said no but that he would go to his car to get it. Not believing this ploy, Loss Prevention told him to come up to the office with them. Sensing police would get involved, he ran but was grabbed by his shirt and started to twist and turn and swung his arms wildly as he tried to flee. One of the employees was struck on the right side of his face but was unharmed. The other employee pushed the juvenile into a magazine rack, and he was handcuffed by them after he fell to the floor.

We took custody of him and transported him to the Youth Division. He had no ID, so we took his word for who he was. There was no digitalized juvenile fingerprinting system in place at this time, and prints were taken manually. His fingerprint card was later visually checked for various loops and swirls by a detective using a magnifying glass for name confirmation until sometime in the mid 1990's when technology performed that task.

We were told the next day by a detective doing follow up that the juvenile had lied to us about his identity because he had escaped from a juvenile detention center, skipped a court date, and had a warrant for Assault.

Deployment officers were driving around on their own with no tasks for the day other than to try to find someone suspicious that they could shadow for a while, something this team of veteran officers was very good at doing at this point in time. One of them had a license plate number checked by a cohort back at the police station and the vehicle returned as stolen. They informed patrol officers of their situation and provided their location. As we arrived, we saw that two suspects had just bailed out of the stolen car and were running from an undercover officer. We quickly reversed and proceeded to the first street past the apartment complex hoping to intercept. I told my partner to slow down and let me out. I ran across a front yard and tried to open a backyard gate, but it was locked. I scrambled around the house and caught a glimpse of one of the suspects running down a driveway having come from the direction of the apartment complex. He noticed me as I noticed him, then he passed behind a large ground level evergreen tree that shielded our view of one another. During that brief period where he had passed behind the tree, his run became a walk as he became visible again on the other side. He was attempting to play innocent bystander in the hopes of eluding me. I encountered him at gunpoint and ordered him to get on the ground. Playing dumb, he asked what was going on and what did he do, but now made no attempt to flee. As he lay down on a driveway, I knelt on his back and cuffed him. I cannot tell the dispatcher that I have one suspect in custody because there was so much radio traffic involving the foot pursuit of the other suspect. I decided to just hold the suspect and wait for a Unit to drive down the street or for radio traffic to slow so I can announce one in custody. The kid was still hoping for freedom and told me that he was just taking a shortcut through somebody's yard. I heard sirens, and another officer drove down my street location and stopped upon having seen me. I had heard "Assist Officer" on the radio a minute before but didn't hear the location. It was for me. A homeowner had seen me kneeling on the suspect for several minutes and assumed that I needed some help. I told the first officer and the dispatcher that I had one suspect in custody and that everything was fine. We took the suspect back to our Patrol Division where the undercover officer who had first made initial contact with the suspects positively identified my prisoner as one of them.

The suspect informed us that he was the nephew of one of our Assistant Police Chief's.

An employee had worked at a large electronics store for a year while he attended a local university well known for its academic excellence. He got a key for the expensive small product cage and removed a miniature Sony Digital Camera valued at $200 from its box. He walked several aisles and then put the camera around his neck (attached strap). After 45 minutes, he took it off his neck and placed it into his dress shirt pocket and walked outside to go to lunch without having paid for it. He was being watched via camera surveillance by Loss Prevention and was detained outside. We took him to jail for his theft. What made him unusual was that his college major was Pre-Law, and that after graduating from Law School he wanted to be a Prosecuting Attorney for a D.A.'s office to seek convictions and put criminals behind bars.

A young woman was released from Terrell Mental Hospital but had no medication. The very next day, her mother had to call police because her daughter was loud and difficult to control. A male neighbor had overheard the commotion and came over to help but was reluctant to touch her after she accused him of being a rapist and a murderer.

We obtained her name from her mother because the name "God" which she gave us was already taken. The daughter agreed to let us take her to PMH (Parkland Mental Hospital) and tried to hug me and kiss me because she was happy to go there. This young lady was gorgeous but was not at all in control of her mental faculties, being manic-depressive, schizophrenic, having severe emotional swings, periodic crying, apologies, and talking to herself in her native language and in English.

After we started our trip, she asked us for some gum or candy or a Slurpee. I told her that we couldn't do that. She politely asked a few more times, and when I saw how backed up the freeway was, I told my partner to go to a 7 Eleven so that I could get her some gum and a Slurpee. When I returned with her goodies she smiled, thanked me, and asked if she could kiss me, leaning toward me and puckering her lips. I thanked her but told her that I could not allow that. She wasn't taking no for an answer. She unfastened her seat belt and leaned over to kiss my right arm as I sat next to her, and the right arm of my driving partner.

I was returning to my division from municipal court and eyed a man meandering down the sidewalk making eye-level gestures with his hands and talking to himself. I suspected that he might be high on drugs and needed to stay at the Detox Inn. I made a U-turn and pulled abreast of him and exited my car. He stopped as I approached him was smiling, seemingly very happy. He was a tall, skinny man with unkempt long hair, browned decayed teeth, wrinkled dirty clothes, and a foul unwashed odor. I asked if he had been using drugs, taking any medication, had any mental or neurotic problems, and his answer to each question was a respectful "No sir", as he kept the grin on his face. I asked him to roll up his sleeves to examine his arms for any needle tracks, but he had none. He was just weird. Sensing my departure, he said in a meek high-pitched voice "Can I have a hug?" I raised my hand as I walked away to say goodbye and told him "Take care!" As I drove by, I waved at him again, but his smile had disappeared and now he looked sad and despondent. I'm sure people rarely engaged him in conversation, and he was lonely. Truth was, if a young mother would've been walking down the sidewalk, she would've herded her kids for protection because of the homeless man's appearance.

A young man was walking with a friend on the bike trail at White Rock Lake. They currently lived at the Salvation Army because the man had a substance abuse problem, which could've been a factor (an altered mental state?) for what was to happen. The two men had tried to get better acquainted with two young women that they had met by talking and joking with them. At one point the young man dared the girls to flash their breasts, but they were unflinching in their desire to keep their shirts on. The young man jokingly asked what it would take to show their boobs, and one girl jokingly replied that he needed to jump off the bridge on which they were walking. The bridge was only about 10-15 feet above the water. The girl never expected the man to take her seriously, but in a flash, he unhesitatingly jumped over the rail into the lake water below. Soon following his lead, the other man did the same, and was quickly on the surface laughing. The first man to jump was soon floundering nearby, screaming for help because he couldn't swim. He mistakenly assumed that the water on this north end of the lake was shallow and not over his head. He soon went under the murky water. Two other lake users climbed over the bridge rail to jump in and assist the frantic friend now also trying to find him. The drowned man was not found until the next day by police divers who recovered him from the lake bottom very near where he had hit the water on his death plunge.

A man parked in his alley driveway and went inside his house through the open overhead door to grab his bagged lunch. During that brief time, he and his wife overheard a noise coming from the garage. When they came out into the open garage, they glimpsed what appeared to be a suspect placing some of the man's tools into the open trunk of a vehicle parked in the alley and then close it. The man grabbed a crowbar and hurried over to the vehicle, accusing the suspect of having just been inside his garage. The suspect denied it and stepped into his vehicle. The homeowner was wielding the crowbar and when he told the suspect to open his trunk, the suspect hit the inside button to pop the trunk. The man told his wife to look in the trunk to see if she could see any of his tools in there. She told him yes. Knowing that the man's attention was diverted to the trunk, the suspect saw his chance to accelerate and flee. The homeowner swung a good blow with his crowbar and shattered the driver side window of the suspect vehicle as it passed by him. It had all happened so fast that neither the husband nor wife got the license plate number, while the suspect got $1500 of tools.

Driving down the road one day, I noticed a large pothole directly in front of my car's right side. Too late to avoid it, I hit it squarely while going about 40mph, and the jostling impact shook loose the hubcap which I watched roll down the road in my rearview mirror. I U-turned and then parked atop the median, walking across the street to retrieve my hubcap. Three days of near constant rain in sub-zero temperatures had created many potholes in the city. Besides my hubcap, there were about 15 others in the grass, all of which resulted from other vehicles hitting the same deep foxhole...er, pothole.

An hour later, we volunteered for what we thought was another routine accident on the same street. A man was speeding in his pickup truck did not have a firm grip on the steering wheel or was distracted and struck the same pothole. He lost control and jumped from the middle lane to the left lane, then over the center median, crossed the oncoming three lanes of traffic, went over a curb, over a bush and flowerbed, struck a wrought iron apartment complex fence, then a parked car facing him on the other side forcing it backwards out of its parking space, then struck another parked car at an angle forcing it to slide over and strike another parked car. What a mess and a long accident report. But laughably according to him he wasn't speeding at the time.

I was driving on the west side of White Rock Lake when I saw a saddled but rider-less horse galloping through the park. I circled around to follow it as he ran on the bike trail and on the road, and I tried to block some small intersections that were in his path. It was a weekday, with little traffic. I followed him to a house with a horse corral in their back yard. The horse had run about a mile to visit a horse friend and stopped to nuzzle. We found the rider and re-united the pair. The rider and a friend had dismounted their horse to talk. A passing bicyclist had spooked the other horse, which reared up on its hind legs. This reaction had frightened the owners' horse, which bolted away in a sprint and ended up at a familiar corral.

A man entered a bank and slid a teller a note that read "This is a gun. Give me all the 50's and 100's". Under obvious duress, the teller hurried and gave him two stacks of bills totaling perhaps $2500 and was about to give him more when the suspect took the note and the money and walked out the front door. I was dispatched on the bank robbery. While I was running Code3 lights and siren, and speeding 85mph, a DPD detective broadcasted to me on the radio the name of the probable suspect. He told me that he will be arriving at the bank shortly with photos of the presumed suspect. Shortly after I arrived and broadcasted a suspect description, the detective arrived along with the FBI. Witnesses fingered the correct suspect in the photos that they were shown. The suspect was wanted for a string of 8 other bank robberies.

The next day I heard that the FBI had obtained his phone number. He was contacted and casually told that he had an income tax refund waiting for him at a particular public address. He was greedy and had been duped. He made an appearance and was promptly arrested by the "actors" in this fabricated skit who were all law enforcement.

On a cold rainy December day, I answered a call about someone having turned in a briefcase at a trailer park office. The manager had already looked inside it, and contacted the owner and discerned that it had been stolen when his car was burglarized. I went over to the dumpster where the briefcase had been found and hoped to recover more stolen property. No luck. As I began to drive away, I decided to run the tag of a blue Cadillac that was near the dumpster. It returned as stolen. I searched the Cadillac and found more stolen property belonging to the man who had his briefcase stolen, including his Passport. I had the Evidence Section come to dust for prints and some good ones were found for processing.

A woman ran out and asked me what was happening, as she had reported her car being stolen that same morning. The suspects had burglarized another vehicle while in the Cadillac, dumped the Cadillac and the briefcase in the trailer park, and then stole the woman's car from just several yards away for a fresh start.

While working a summer-time Violent Crime Task Force one night, I reviewed the calls that were holding and volunteered for a Signal 40, or "Other" that was only one block away. An anonymous person reported that they observed a rifle being transferred from one vehicle to another and provided the vehicle info inside which the rifle now rested. I spotted the vehicle in a tavern parking lot and looked inside while shining my flashlight from the outside. All that I saw was an aluminum baseball bat lying on the rear floorboard. I thought that maybe the caller had just thought that it was a rifle, but I still took another officer inside the bar to search for the vehicle owner. I had the DJ make an announcement over his microphone for the owner of the vehicle to step outside, which he soon did. I told him in the low lighting that our caller may have thought that his bat was a rifle. I asked if he had anything in the trunk, and he replied that he wasn't trying to hide anything. He opened his trunk with me and the other officer flanking him. To our surprise, there was an SKS 7.62mm Assault Rifle lying atop some other items. The owner lied and told us that he forgot that it was there. I asked him if it was loaded, and he quietly said that he didn't know. For safety reasons, I picked it up and pulled the bolt back. It was loaded, as a bullet popped out of the ejection port. I pulled the bolt back 8 more times, and each time a round ejected. A serial number check of the weapon showed that it was not stolen. The reserved owner informed us that he only had it for protection, as he had received death threats before, but was reluctant to elaborate. I advised him that he could carry that weapon in his trunk but recommended that a better place for it was in his home. Given his somewhat secretive non-disclosure of all the facts surrounding his need to carry the rifle, I documented the situation with an Incident Report with his name and vehicle information in case it became relevant in the future.

I was on my way to work in uniform one morning with my window partly down. I sniffed what I thought was the faint scent of marijuana, but then thought that maybe I was imagining it because I had a small marijuana arrest from the day before. The rush hour traffic gridlock started moving again and I detected a larger whiff of burning marijuana. I looked around to see which of the nearby cars had a window down, and saw only one, so I knew that it had to be him. I'd forgotten that I was wearing my police hand-held radio (we checked them out each day but just the previous day we were each issued our own), so I called 911 on my cell phone. I gave the operator the circumstance, direction, and the suspect and vehicle details and continued to follow him. It took a few miles, but a co-worker caught up with us and stopped the dope smoker's vehicle. I stepped out of my car to cover him and watched the male driver while the other officer opened the driver door to begin his search for the marijuana. There in plain view between the driver door and the driver seat was a clear baggie of weed. The suspect was handcuffed, and his car was towed. He told me that he had seen me in his rearview mirror. I had a feeling that he may have, so I didn't always follow him from his lane, and many times I smiled as I was on the phone with the 911 clerk to allay any suspicions he may have had about my following him. The arrested man was upset, asking me why I did that because he was just on his way to work (while high?). He had a child safety seat in the back, and I pondered if he ever smoked weed while his daughter was in the car.

One minute I was placing an orange 24HR tow sticker on a car that had been left on the shoulder of a road for a few days, and the next I had two guys race up to stop behind my squad car to tell me that a burglar was walking down the street behind me. I announced the murky details and street location to the dispatcher, and some officers started driving my way. I spied the man that I had been told about and stopped to get out, ordering him to get his hands up. As I searched the man, he nonchalantly reached into his left coat pocket and pulled out a kitchen knife with a six-inch blade and simultaneously said "I have this in my pocket." I snatched it away from him and tossed it onto my front seat, then handcuffed him just as another officer had arrived. I had him watch my arrestee and had another officer look for a TV and a microwave that the two men who flagged me down said was by a business dumpster. He found them there. I had him check the serial numbers with NCIC to see if the items had been reported stolen, but they had no record. I drove a nearby apartment complex to maybe get lucky and see a burglarized apartment, or have someone flag me down about one, but that did not occur. The arrestee's story was that he was taking a shortcut, found the property by the dumpster, and called his brother-in-law for a ride. He arrived with a friend but would not let my arrestee put the items into his vehicle and drove off. The arrestee put the items down and tried to follow them on foot because he still needed a ride home. A short time later, the two men saw me and told me of their suspicions. We never did find a burglarized residence, and no burglary calls were in the queue of calls to be dispatched. I brought the arrestee to jail for UCW (Unlawful Carry Weapon) for possessing a knife blade over the legal 3.5-inch length. The TV and microwave were placed in the property room as Found Property.

The next day when I was off, another officer who was present at the scene to assist me found a burglary offense report with the above property having been stolen. The owner was at work and made the report after she returned home, which was after we had already ended our shift. My arrestee who was still in jail was then charged with the burglary too.

My first rookie and I had just taken a robbery report from a complainant at a bit past 8pm. We were driving him around in the back seat hoping to spot the vehicle with the four suspects. As we were returning, we saw a vehicle backed into a parking space, but couldn't tell how many males were inside. We stopped and stepped out to investigate. The driver door was open with the window down. We both smelled marijuana and had the driver step out of the vehicle, as well as the two others that were inside. After we patted them down for weapons, I searched the vehicle. I didn't find any marijuana but did find a loaded .357 Magnum revolver under the driver seat. We placed the 17-year-old driver under arrest for UCW. The other two males had no warrants and were released when the robbery victim still in our police cruiser told us that these males did not rob him. The driver was searched, and a small baggie of weed was found in the little pocket of his right blue jean pants pocket. The mother of our arrestee appeared, and we informed her of our actions and the reason for her son's arrest. She at first alluded to our having planted a weapon to frame her son. After I explained that no officer was going to spend hundreds of dollars on a pistol only to have to put it in the property room for evidence to frame anybody, and her son wasn't charged with the robbery, just possession of the pistol and MJ, she dropped the subject. She confronted her son as he sat in our vehicle, and he admitted to her ashamedly that it was his gun. We did not tow the arrestee vehicle and released it to the mother.

A bank robbery had just occurred, and I was first on the scene, having only been about a mile away. I quickly spoke to witnesses to broadcast a suspect and vehicle description as well as a direction of travel. The two suspects had walked inside together and then split up. One loitered in the customer waiting area, while the other slipped a teller a note that informed her that he had a gun, though she never saw one. The teller began filling a canvas bank bag with cash, and calmly tried to smoothly slide the suspect note toward her to keep it for evidence. The suspect grabbed the note and the bank bag and both he and his accomplice ran out the front door. As they did, they passed a couple that had just parked and were walking toward the entrance. They correctly concluded that two males running out of a bank carrying a canvas bank bag just didn't look right and memorized the license plate of the fleeing suspect vehicle. The bank manager smartly had all the witnesses who saw the suspects write a separate statement about what they remembered about them. Other officers had trailed the stolen cash in a vehicle, but it was a different vehicle than what I had broadcast. The vehicle was stopped but the DPD and FBI wondered if they had the right suspect because he wore a different shirt and didn't appear to be the race that I had initially said on the radio. One witness thought that one suspect was of a different race, and that was who they had in custody. A search of his vehicle revealed the stolen bag of cash. This suspect was positively identified as one of the bank robbers when I transported the witnesses to the location. One suspect was still at large, though he had no loot. The suspects had taken care to hatch a plan involving switching vehicles expecting to improve their odds of evasion and foil the police. Questionable with one bank robbery suspect arrested and one still on the run.

While I was walking outside at an apartment complex on a call, a young woman walked over and handed me a small Dallas

PD badge that she had found on the ground. It had a small hole in it like it had been a pendant on a chain. There was also a badge number on it. I called downtown and gave them my credentials so that they could look up the officer to whom it belonged to enable me to return it. It belonged to an officer who had been killed in an off-duty accident months before. I returned it to his appreciative brother who was also a DPD officer.

Because of personal experience, some police officers detest and loathe some types of criminals more than others. For example, no one likes a bully or some young kid who acts tough and defiant to an adult authority figure, be it parent, teacher, or police.

We were very busy one day with a dozen calls holding. My two partners took their bicycles downtown for some repairs in preparation for the World Cup games to be played in Dallas in 1994. I decided that while I waited for their return, I could ease the burden of patrol officers by taking a patrol car to answer a few quick calls and be done before my partners returned. I took a call that was 2 ½ hours old involving some kid that refused to leave a 7-Eleven store. He had to be gone, 2 ½ hours had passed. Nope. The 14-year-old kid was still inside the store harassing customers by trying to sell them oven mitts and candy for some junior enterprise program. When the owner told the kid to leave before, the kid had said "I'm not going anywhere, you can't tell me what to do. I'm staying." The audacity of this punk unnerved me. I confronted the kid, and I told him that the owner had every right to tell him to leave, it was his store! Why should the owner allow you to compete with him by selling your candy here when he has candy of his own to sell? He had no business sucking up the air conditioning on this hot day, he needed to be outside somewhere else meeting people, and that he had no right to be there in the 7-Eleven as a competitor. He then asked me what would happen if he didn't leave. I told him that I would arrest him for criminal trespassing and take him to our Youth Division. He candidly admitted and almost boasted that he had been there before. "I'm sure you have" I shot back. I had the manager/owner come over to ask the boy to leave in my presence. I then firmly told the juvenile "Now beat it! Get out of here!' If you come back to the store or their parking lot, you'll be arrested!" He left without incident or any backtalk. I left with the thought that some kids just lacked discipline because few people told them that their actions and decisions had consequences and that they were pretty much doing whatever they wanted with no structure or boundaries or rules set by their parent(s).

I performed a vehicle license plate check on my computer and saw that a vehicle ahead of me had several traffic ticket warrants. I conducted a traffic stop some thirty yards from a bus stop where six people were waiting, and now watching my every move, a live cop in action. With their eyes upon me, I had to do my best to be professional and take care of business. I determined that the driver was indeed the person with the outstanding warrants, so with a quick phone call I confirmed that the warrants were valid. I approached his vehicle, had him exit, informed him that he was being placed under arrest, and swiftly slapped on the handcuffs. I searched him and brought him to the passenger side of the squad car. The door was locked. No problem, I'll just hit the driver side door unlock button. It too was locked. Momentary panic set in. But hey, I have a spare key in my pants pocket. I shoved my hand into my pocket but the only spare that I had was change. Gulp. Are the bus stop people still watching? Yes. It's time to be embarrassed. Daylight, doors locked, engine running, red and blue lights revolving, handcuffed prisoner. Nice going butthead. Thankfully I had a handheld radio at my side and contacted the station to have another officer bring me a key. I had accidentally hit the vertical door lock button which was right behind the door handle cavity. It was a design flaw. This happened to other officers a few times a week. When someone with a large hand pulled open the door handle, and then pushed the door open using the same hand, the wrist would bend and sometimes inadvertently strike the lock/unlock button.

Murphy's Law being what it is, as I waited with my handcuffed prisoner a neighbor stepped out of a small credit union just on the other side of the bus stop and walked over to greet me. He informed me that all the girls inside had leaned over to look through a window to see what was happening after I had arrested the driver, meaning they had seen the whole thing. Wonderful. Now even more people knew what a nincompoop I had been.

Three of us went to an apartment complex office for a shots-fired call where two males were seen with guns and had walked back inside an apartment. We went to the office and learned that two apartments were involved, one vacant and one occupied. We used a key to enter the vacant unit first and found a 6'2", 235lb. male with three teardrop tattoos by his left eye sleeping on the carpeted floor in a sleeping bag. There were even some furniture items and some kitchen chairs and a table. We rousted him and he was handcuffed. A subject check showed that he had some ticket warrants. They were confirmed, and I remained with him while the other two officers checked on the other Unit.

I was beginning to wonder what was taking them so long when I heard one of them ask the dispatcher to check the serial numbers of some weapons to ascertain if they were stolen (they were not). Minutes later, the officer returned to my apartment carrying an AK-47 assault rifle with a pistol grip and mounted scope and a 12-gauge Mossberg shotgun. They had gone to the occupied apartment and a woman came to the door. They explained that there had been reports of drugs and weapons in her apartment, and she consented to allow them to come inside and take a gander. While one officer watched her and four males, the other searched the apartment and returned to her with these two weapons that he had found. The nervous woman was asked if the weapons belonged to her and if she wanted them. Probably sensing an easy way to get rid of these guns and keep them away from the four males, she replied "No. You take them!" They were brought to our Property Room. This ended the reports that management had been getting from tenants about shots fired in the complex and from their balcony.

Many times, when responding to an accident scene we would not check the drivers for warrants, and just focused on the accident report and clearing the scene. One time though I thought that both males had the appearance (yes, I judged a book by its cover) of having outstanding warrants. One did not, but the other motorist had a DL picture that just screamed "druggie" to me. Sure enough, he had a felony Meth warrant, and I took him to jail. I was surprised that he was a cooperative, happy-go-lucky guy with a great attitude and sense of humor.

On a hot day a suspect knocked on an apartment door and asked if he could have a glass of water. As the mother or one of her children were fetching him a glass of water, the suspect seized upon a crime of opportunity which had presented itself. He grabbed the woman's nearby purse and ran out the door, leaving behind his stinky slippers that he had kindly removed outside the front door prior to walking inside.

A day-and-a-half later, the complainant saw the purse thief at a nearby 7-Eleven store and called the police. I showed up, and the woman came running over to me to point out the suspect as he was walking away. I called the suspect over and then handcuffed him. He had none of her property on his person, and nothing of hers was recovered. I met the woman back at her apartment and then had her children look at the suspect. They also nodded in agreement that he was the thief who stole their mother's purse. As I was leaving, the woman came over and handed me the suspect's slippers, stating that he had left them there when he fled. He denied that they belonged to him, but the slipper stink odor matched his own odor, so he got to keep them. He did not cooperate with a detective back at the police station and I took him to jail. There, his fingerprints from previous arrests revealed his identity and he was positively identified by his arrest record photos.

I drove up into an apartment complex for a Dead Person call, or a "Signal 27" as it is known in Dallas. Even in the parking lot, I could smell the putrid stench of death, not unlike the smell of a decomposing animal alongside the road. The firemen had already gone inside the apartment, and confirmed what I already knew. They had worn their gas masks and one wrongly estimated that the man had been dead for more than 30 days. Before they departed, they were kind enough to ask if I had wanted to use their headgear to avoid the disgusting odor, but I declined.

The manager told me that she had sent a maintenance man to the deceased tenant's unit because his rent was ten days overdue. When he placed the overdue rent notice on the man's front door, he noticed the powerful odor and the many flies that were eagerly looking for a way in from the front door. I contacted the man's employer and found out that he was a waiter, but he had not worked in almost two weeks. I went to the apartment and just before I stepped inside, I inhaled a deep lung full of semi-good air. I entered and saw the complainant lying on the carpet on his side just behind a bedroom couch, his white skin having turned a brownish-green color. I didn't quite make it out of the apartment while holding my breath and was forced to exhale and take a gulp of air as I exited, nearly activating my gag reflex.

The Medical Examiner and the Physical Evidence Tech arrived and entered without the aid of Vick's VapoRub under their noses. They commented that the smell would have been much worse and the body more decomposed had it been the scorching summertime instead of the second week in April. A friend of the deceased appeared and stated that they used to be roommates, and that he was depressed and despondent and had spoken of killing himself on a few occasions. There was an empty 50 capsule Valium bottle on the kitchen counter. The dead man was probably affected by the overdose sooner than he had expected; I doubt that he had planned on being found naked.

At about 2 a.m. one late August night, I did a license plate of the vehicle in front of me and saw that someone driving that vehicle had traffic warrants from another city. I made a traffic stop as I neared her vehicle and before I even said a word I heard "You must not have anything better to do tonight!" I asked her if she had an attitude. She smirked and replied that she was just being sarcastic but that she DID have an attitude. I saw that her DL name was the same as on the unpaid traffic ticket warrants and said that she would be taken to jail and her car would be towed. "Go right ahead!" she retorted. As I was checking her DL on my laptop, I saw that it was suspended and that she had another warrant from another city. The motorist stepped out of her vehicle and began walking across the parking lot. I jumped from my cruiser and ran over to ask her where she thought that she was going. She said that she was going to use the phone (pay phones at this time). I told her that she needed to go back and wait by her car. "I'm going to use the phone! I'm a grown woman, I'm an adult. You can't tell me what to do!" I raised my voice and told her that she was being lawfully detained, and she wasn't free to walk away just because she felt like it, that she couldn't leave until I gave her permission to do so. She didn't move, and just looked at me with scorn and contempt. I told her to go back to wait by her car. She was still unmoved and uncooperative. I grabbed her by her arm and escorted her back to her vehicle and told her to remain there and to not walk away. The other officer arrived as I requested, the motorist was arrested when the warrants were confirmed, and her vehicle was towed.

A friend went to visit a buddy one morning. As he was walking toward the motorhome, he detected a foul odor and feared the worst. Sure enough, when he peered inside the vehicle, he saw his friend lying on his back in the darkened aisle way, rotting in the 100-degree heat. The corpse had been there just two days, but the rate of decomposition had accelerated from the heat and unsanitary living conditions, with roaches and flies already present at the time of his passing.

I arrived to find the Fire Department already on scene, as well as a couple of police officers, but no officer had yet entered the metal tomb. I volunteered, and a fireman strapped me on an oxygen tank and mask, and I clambered inside. The mask has a good tight seal, and I could not detect any body stench, but the sight of the deceased' bloated cracked belly with bugs crawling all over it made me uncomfortable about possibly inadvertently bringing some of those bugs to my home when my shift was over, so I backed out to exit. I had noticed a shotgun at the front driver compartment, and heard that the old, retired Air Force Colonel was a bit paranoid about someone trying to steal or disturb his three tarp-covered luxury cars outside and often posted watch over them. He owned a pistol and a rifle as well and had been known to ever so occasionally squeeze off a warning shot if he thought someone got too close to his prized possessions. The side door was open an inch when the friend arrived, which explained the variety of creepy crawlers that I saw. The deceased had open heart surgery two years before and hadn't been very active. He was too bloated and cumbersome to be pulled out the front door, so an axe was wielded by a fireman to force entry into the larger locked side door. This made him more accessible to the Medical Examiner who was on his way. When the side door was torn off bringing light inside, a swarm of cockroaches scattered from under a pile of accumulated debris that had been stacked against the inside of the unused door. With each successive raking of the pile to clear a pathway for the removal of the deceased, another swarm of cockroaches scurried away.

I was shocked that this man would tolerate living conditions like this in his declining years. His retired military officer's pension afforded him the expense of an occasional maid and/or cook. Instead, he let his weak heart, shortness of breath, and obesity overrule his need for a sanitary home.

A man who was practicing his archery skills by a RR track waved us down. He said that as he was practicing, a homeless man walked out of the woods nearby and began to voice his distaste and displeasure for police officers (he had seen us ride by). Having shared his thoughts, he went back into the woods.

Little did he know that the archer with whom he spoke was an off-duty Deputy Sheriff.

Having been informed of this non-supporter and knowing that he must have had an illegal shack in the woods, we went to investigate his campsite that was supposedly 20 yards from the wooded edge. I was riding a police bicycle that day and was wearing shorts as I entered the wooded area. The campsite was just a wet gym bag full of damp clothes and a damp sleeping bag on a plastic tarp, but there was no sign of the homeless man. Shortly afterward, we went to lunch at Chili's. My first stop was the restroom, where I washed my hands AFTER I used the urinal. Days later, I wished that I had washed them immediately upon entering the men's room. Had I done so, I would've avoided the embarrassing location of my poison ivy outbreak.

An Indecent Exposure suspect was entertaining delusions of grandeur when he surreptitiously left a secret admirer note on his victim's door. She found it when she returned home from work: "Hello. I know that you don't know me but I need to say it anyway. Dem (sic) your (sic) fine! I think your (sic) beautyful (sic). I'd like to meet you but I'm way to shy. I think you are very sexy! I'll see you when I see you. Your fantasy invisible man."

His believing that she would be flattered by this note and not afraid after he had exposed himself to her is the real fantasy here.

We arrived for a domestic disturbance reported by a neighbor, but no one came to the door despite out repeated knocks. All was quiet, so we started to descend to the parking lot. At the stairway bottom, there was an 18yr old girl with some clothes and property in the breezeway. I asked her if she lived in Apartment #1214, but rather than tell me "No", she responded with a "Why"? Now I knew that she was in the apartment earlier. I inquired about a fight. She said that she had one with her boyfriend, but that he would never hit her, it was just verbal. We waited outside with her as she loaded her property into her car. Her boyfriend that had ignored our knocks now stepped out onto the second-floor balcony and used a utility knife to scratch his wrist to get her attention and concern. I shouted up to him "What're you doing?" "Nothing" was his reply. I asked if he often self-mutilated himself, and he said, "No sir". "Get back inside" I commanded, and he apologized and complied. I told my partner what he had done, and we went back upstairs, and the door was unlocked. The girl walked inside before us—unafraid—knowing that he was not a threat to her, only himself. I walked in behind her, and he was not expecting to see me. He was holding the utility knife to his throat. I demanded that he put the knife down, and he apologized and immediately tossed the knife to the floor. I handcuffed him, and we transported him to get some psychological help. Along the way, I chatted with him a bit. He seemed like a good kid. His girlfriend was a trust fund baby and didn't have to work. She spent much of her time partying, hanging out with friends, and doing drugs while he worked. Today he came home early from work and found her having sex on their bed with his best friend. Rather than admit fault or beg him for forgiveness, her twisted logic caused her to denigrate him. In her mind, If he hadn't come home early, none of that would have ever happened and everything would've been just fine. I told him that she was beautiful, but crazy, and couldn't be trusted. He needed to save his dignity and pride and stop groveling to her, he could do better and find someone who appreciated him because she clearly did not.

He probably tried to get her back just as soon as he came home from the hospital.

Two people were standing on shoreline rocks trying to get some good lake photos. One of them saw something unusual several feet away and walked over to get a closer look. It was a hairless white torso without any limbs or a head. It had been in the water for a week or two and was decomposing.

Upon seeing it, I contacted Homicide, Crime Scene, and the Medical Examiner's office but expressed some doubts about whether it was a human body. The first two decided to let the Medical Examiner look first before they came out and asked me to keep them informed. The M.E. put on her waterproof booties and stepped into the lake and saw a couple of tufts of hair and started to think that it was not a human body. She picked it up with her rubber-gloved hands and turned it over to reveal a face. The face was clearly that of a large beaver.

I stopped a motorist for a burned-out left brake light. I recognized him. He showed me the paperwork that he had paid to an attorney to take care of the ticket that I had written him 10 days earlier at the same place, direction, and time. He received a warning.

We had just finished eating when we were dispatched on a call concerning a neighbor who had phoned police regarding a strange car in his neighbor's driveway. They were out-of-town, no one was supposed to be there, and a light was on in the house. We were directed by a sergeant to position ourselves at opposite sides of a wooden fence that encircled the yard. Our weapons were at our sides, ready to confront the burglar that might emerge at any moment. In minutes, our police helicopter was circling overhead with its bright spotlight illuminating the house and occasionally me as it continued to fly in circles. I was five yards from a fairly busy road and motorists could see my back as they passed by, my pistol at my side. Some slowed down to get a better look, while others accelerated. After the low-flying loud helicopter circled overhead a dozen times, the pilot broke away and surged into the darkness and disappeared. I was perplexed. My partner told me on the radio to return to our car. Officers had gone to the front door and the man inside answered. He was the uncle of one of the homeowners and had agreed to take care of a few things while they were gone. An exhilarating start to this call suddenly had a dull end.

I was typing a report on my computer when an officer told the dispatcher that he had a car that was not stopping for him and added that he was "in chase". I was only a few blocks away, but by the time I got out of the neighborhood to the major street where the chase had been, it was too late, they had already passed. I followed and maneuvered to conform to the chase on the radio, hoping to parallel it and be lucky enough to intercept it. The suspect struck a parked car in a neighborhood, then exited and scrambled over a fence and ran across a road. Two officers spotted him run down an alley. I just happened to turn a corner as they said that and was able to turn in behind them as they entered that alley. We stopped and got out of our cars to search some backyards. They had not seen which yard the suspect had entered, but he had to be in our proximity. I jumped over a fence and drew my weapon to the scan position. I searched an open shed, but he wasn't there. I hopped back over the alley fence in time and saw that another officer had located the suspect and handcuffed him and was now walking back toward me. I watched as the suspect shorts—already worn halfway down his buttocks—dropped down to his ankles, revealing his red boxer shorts underwear. He reeked of marijuana, and I remarked to him that he had marijuana in his car. "Yes sir" was his respectful reply. I had him sit down on someone's rear driveway while the other officer retrieved his police cruiser. An ambulance had been called because he had some minor scrapes on his knees and a shoulder in his futile attempt to elude capture. They arrived and quickly just poured some hydrogen peroxide on his minor scuffs and were back on their way. As we were waiting to get picked up, the suspect began to berate and disparage himself. He said "Man, I do some of the most stupid shit! I can't believe I did that! I'm always messin' up! That was stupid! I want to apologize to you guys! I'm sorry man! I'm sorry I put you guys through this!" Any officer will tell you that such a coherent admission of guilt by a suspect at the scene of the crime is rare. I responded that we appreciated his apology, but that he would be suffering the consequences of his actions. The car this 21-year-old had driven belonged to his mother. The original officer found marijuana and crack cocaine inside of it during his vehicle search. This felonious chain of events all happened simply because the suspect didn't want to get a ticket for not having had a driver license. The officer probably would have initiated a vehicle search because of the marijuana odor and found the drugs anyway, but the suspect wouldn't have had the felony evading police charge had he simply stopped for the officer.

I saw the homeowners step out their back door and stand by their fence; they were curious about all the commotion on the other side of their driveway. I smiled and commented "I'm just guessing here, but I'm thinking that this is probably the first time that a handcuffed man has sat on your driveway with his pants around his ankles, am I right"? They both cracked a smile and the man said, "Yes officer, this is the first time."

A woman told her boyfriend about a man that was driving a white Chevy PU truck that had followed a short distance and then approached her while she was walking in the park and asked her if she might like to get to know him better. Now she saw him in another park, facing a playground about 50 yards away with children playing in it. Her boyfriend noticed that the man was looking at a porn magazine and seemed to be shaking a bit as if he might be masturbating. I arrived to find that they were both in white Chevy PU trucks and parked in adjacent parking spaces. The boyfriend spoke to me from his truck and told me that the suspect had just thrown his magazine behind his seat when I pulled into the parking lot. I strolled over to the suspect truck and pointedly asked if he had any nudie magazines. He replied yes and when I asked him where it was, he told me that it was behind the seat and retrieved it for me. I quickly flipped through it to be sure that it wasn't child pornography, or concealing child pornography. I candidly told him that whatever he was thinking about doing here while looking at sex magazines in a park where children were playing needed to be done at home, not in a public place. He never once asked me why I was questioning him, so I was sure that he had been fondling and stroking himself for pleasure whether his penis was exposed or not.

I told the boyfriend after the suspect departed that I would be doing a Suspicious Person report and make sure that it was forwarded to sexual assaults, our Fusion Unit (like a DPD data center), our Intelligence Unit, and Child Exploitation. The man thanked me and extended his hand, but I told him with a smile that I had handled the suspect's girlie mag and was better off not touching him.

My partner was looking to see what calls were holding to see if we could take a nearby call. We found one, a Hit & Run on the same street where we were driving. He looked up on time to see that a woman was waving us down. I stopped and she told us that a woman with long hair driving a black Jaguar had struck the left side of her car, then immediately fled the scene via a church parking lot. She didn't think that she could recognize the woman if she saw her again. We were wondering why the driver of a Jaguar wouldn't stop, because we knew that the vehicle must be insured given its hefty value. The motorist did write down the suspect license plate, and the registration returned to an address not far away. The woman added that she was sorry, but she couldn't wait around as she had a two hour meeting to attend. We assured her that wasn't a problem and told her that we would obtain the driver and insurance info from the registered address and get back with her.

At the suspect vehicle address, a long-haired 14-year-old boy answered the door. I asked if we could speak to one of his parents, and he went to get his dad. His dad was about 70 years old. I inquired about the whereabouts of his Jaguar, and he said that it was in the garage. As we all strolled down the hallway, the boy commented "It was here the last time I looked", fueling our suspicions that he was the driver. Lo and behold, the Jaguar had damage to the right front headlight, the point of impact in our minor accident. I asked the boy if he had been driving the vehicle at the time of the accident, and he respectfully replied, "No sir." I stated that I had been an officer for 20 years, and my partner for 22 years, and that we weren't born yesterday. I added that we wanted to settle this the easy way and just have two drivers exchange information from a minor accident, since no one was hurt. We told him it was just a civil matter, that it only became illegal when someone left the scene of an accident. We didn't want to charge anyone with a Hit and Run accident, and that we had not even spoke to our accident witnesses yet (we didn't have any). Now, I'm going to ask you one more time. Who was driving this vehicle? "I was sir" the boy responded. I had dad retrieve the insurance info and I wrote it down to give to our other driver at her house later, as she lived nearby. The other officer commented to the dad that he was taking this pretty well. He replied that we had not left yet. We left and circled the block to be back on our way and already we saw that the boy had left the house and was walking down the street. We doubted that the grandfather-aged father had any real control over his teenage son, and wondered if there were any real consequences for his unauthorized driving.

At White Rock Lake, many bicyclists rode on the road and knew that state law required them to stop at stop signs. It was a good habit to stop because occasionally officers at the lake would write a citation when instructed because of citizen complaints. I observed one cyclist from about 50 yards away fly downhill and turn left without stopping at the sign. I pulled alongside of him and told him from my squad car that he needed to stop at stop signs, and that if he returned to stop at the stop sign, I would not write him a ticket. I was surprised by his response when he told me "I guess you can write me a ticket." I stopped and walked over to him, remarking that I was not expecting that answer. He retorted "What's the difference if I went back and stopped at the stop sign now? I already ran it. It doesn't change anything. I still ran it. It's just a way for you to show your authority."

I thought for a few moments, and probably surprised him when I said "True. That's true." He commented that he had seen officers writing tickets to bicyclists, but not to vehicles. I asked him if he had ever seen a traffic stop at the lake, and he had no reply. He cockily told a couple of passing cyclists that they were going too fast and that they needed to watch their speed as I was writing him his ticket. Personally, I would have gone back to stop at the stop sign to avoid receiving a citation even if it seemed illogical.

I did a traffic stop for an expired registration. The 21-year-old driver was completely respectful, addressing me with "Yes sir" and "No sir" the whole time. His ID was flagged by the computer with a warning for being a known criminal gang member. I had only written him one of a possible two citations, and upon my return asked him if he was still active in a gang. If someone did belong to a gang, he usually wouldn't deny it and admit to their affiliation as a badge of honor and pride. He said that he didn't do that anymore and pointed to his months-old son in the child safety seat. "Yes sir" and "No sir" to the end of our conversation, he finished by thanking me for my courtesy and told me to be careful. He had transformed himself from a rowdy, reckless past to being a responsible, respectful young man.

I was working overtime on my day off, 5 a.m. to 9 a.m. I stopped at a 7-Eleven, needing and wanting a cup of coffee. There was a chubby girl standing at the front of the store wearing a cowboy hat, tight jeans, and a revealing pink blouse. I saw that she had scratches on her face, like she had been in a fight or had walked into branches. I reached for the door handle to enter and looked her way. She said "Hola", and a brief conversation began and quickly ended after a quick greeting and learning each other's names. I stepped inside, and she followed me. She smiled at me and asked if I could buy her a cappuccino and if I could take her home. It was then that I realized that her eyes were bloodshot, and her breath reeked of alcohol. I inquired about her facial scratches, and she told me that she had been in a fight at a local bar with another girl and was thrown out. She started to say my name a few times. I asked her where she was from and asked about her address. I just wanted it for the Detox form, but she probably thought that I was going to take her home. She was persistent about the cappuccino, so I bought her one. She didn't speak English, so right in front of her I asked the dispatcher on my radio to have a one-man meet me to help me transport a female to Detox. She asked me where the bathroom was, so I pointed to it. She wanted me to go with her and got close to me and smiled. I coyly said "Sexo?" and she smiled and said "Si", then walked over to the bathroom door. She stared at me and smiled, waiting for me, but I was just buying time and smiled back. After a minute, she went inside without me. The other officer arrived while she was still busy. She returned and we let her have a bit more time to enjoy her cappuccino, but she wasn't in much of a hurry. I started to handcuff her, but she thought that I was playing and started grinning. When she realized that it was for real, she began to cry, and tears rolled down her face as she asked us to just take her home. I told her that we couldn't do that. She was angry with me and felt betrayed. I was kind to her, but I had a job to do. She was Publicly Intoxicated, and the truth was that I wasn't sure how much "activity" (our jargon for "Police work") I would have during my short and quiet overtime shift hours.

At Sam's Club, a handicapped man rolled over to me in a wheelchair and told me that he could not park in a handicapped spot in the parking lot because they were all being used, and he told me of two vehicles that did not have a handicapped placard on the rearview mirror nor a handicapped license plate. In short order, I saw that these vehicles were in violation, and I wrote two handicapped violator tickets and placed them under the windshield wiper. I went back inside and waited for the violators to probably come into the store and speak to me. They both did (It was a $500 ticket).

I walked outside with a husband and wife and showed them where they were parked. The handicapped sign was to his immediate left as he stepped out of their car. The woman commented that he had just got out of the hospital (I could see that he had black-and-blue bruising under his eyes) and added that "he can't see very well." I simply asked her if that was the case, then why wasn't she driving? She had no reply. I told her that unless they could produce a handicapped placard, I would not void the ticket. They drove off with the "couldn't see very well" husband still behind the wheel.

The other driver came in to speak with me. I walked out and told and showed him that he had parked on the cross-lined space that was part of the handicapped space. He had an "Honorary Consul" license plate, and I told him then he should be able to get the ticket dismissed in court, but that unless he produced a handicapped placard, I was not going to void his ticket. He didn't like this and walked inside with the ticket in his hand. I correctly sensed that he wanted to speak to a manager and thwarted that desire when I told him that the store manager cannot do anything about his citation because it was a violation of state law. He replied that he didn't see it, and that he was a regular shopper. I told him that a real handicapped person told me about his vehicle, and that he had to park somewhere else as a result. He said that he understood, and that I was right, but then added that writing him a ticket "was extreme". I replied that I was doing my job, and maybe he should make a court date to see if a judge thought that I was "being extreme". He advised me that I was just abusing my authority by advising him to go to court, that he knew that. I told him that he had already said that I was "right" earlier, and if he understood why I wrote the ticket then why were we even having this conversation? Not being authorized to park where he did, he had no further reason to prolong our discussion, and walked out disgusted.

Some criminal offenses are hard to hear and hard to write, especially when it concerns a young child who was sexually abused by an adult (who is often a relative) or even by another child. This instance of pedophilia became known by the interactions of the innocent victim with his father and may be difficult to read.

A father had custody of his child several times each month. They were lying on the bed watching TV at night when the little 5-year-old boy grabbed his dad's hand and casually placed it atop his own genitals. His dad pulled his hand away and told him "No!" He did it again in the same minute to again be sternly told, "NO!" by his father. The father thought the actions to be suspicious, and realized in the morning when his son did it one more time that his son had to have been getting sexually abused. He questioned his son to see if anybody played with him down there. The boy said "yes", and with more questions the father found out that it was from two relatives, a boy slightly older and a teen male who legally was an adult. He also had his son tell him that they took off his underwear and "They bite it." More gentle questioning by dad revealed that the older teen uncle "put it in my mouth and put it in my butt." When asked if he did anything else, his 5-year-old son said, "He pee-pee on me."

I arrived and listened to what had transpired between the father and son. I had to ascertain for myself what had been uncovered by dad in his talk with his son to be sure that there were no leading questions or coaxing or suggestions for answers. The little boy had some reticence about speaking with me until dad told him that it was okay. I had to be sure what the "it" referred to from the sexual assault, and the boy indicated with his nickname for a penis, one with which his dad was familiar. The father felt compelled to tell me that a couple years ago his Ex had told him of the possibility that the slightly older boy who was one of the abusers of his son had possibly been targeted for sexual abuse himself. His Ex ignored the rumor because she didn't want to confront the family and endure any friction as a result. This head-in-the-sand attitude of course did nothing to halt any sexual abuse if it had been happening. The father also relayed to me that the teenage uncle abuser/suspect had babysat for both his son and the slightly older boy on several occasions. I contacted the Child Abuse Unit and made sure that the father had a printed copy of my Offense Report to present to the CPS worker that he was to meet with the next morning.

I had just returned to my squad car after having responded to a call when a woman on a pay phone several feet away began talking to me. She had a cute daughter of about four with pigtails standing beside her. As I was speaking with this woman, I glanced over at the little girl and smiled, and she reciprocated. I continued conversing with the mother when unexpectedly without warning the girl quickly bent down and pulled her pants and underwear down to her ankles. This was followed by her standing upright, staring at me with a bright cheery smile, and holding a forefinger to her lip. Momma was still talking to me and hadn't noticed. I interrupted her and asked her to look at her daughter. Because she was standing beside her daughter from an elevated position, she couldn't see why I had said that. I saw the quandary on her face and added that she should take a step back and look at her daughter again. She did so and smiled at me embarrassingly, then pulled up her daughter's pants.

I viewed this incident at the time as likely something that the little girl learned from some older kids or siblings to get a laugh and gain some acceptance, but in retrospect there was no guarantee that this wasn't a learned behavior that preceded sexual abuse.

I rode my bicycle up to a picnic table at the lake because I saw a beer bottle atop it, and an unleashed Pit Bull scampering around. I knew that I would be writing at least two tickets in this group of four people. There were two females sitting down at the picnic table, one male standing at the table end nearest the beer bottle, and another male further away watching his dog from a distance. As I rode up, the man near the beer stood between me and his beer bottle, blocking my view in the hopes that I hadn't seen it. I informed him that alcohol was illegal in all city parks in Dallas, and I told the other male that his dog needed to be on a leash. I told the man by the beer that I needed to see his I.D. Almost all my stories have been race-neutral because unless race was part of a conversation, it is irrelevant. This was different. One of the women mouthed off at me and declared "Oh! I see how it is! You see a black man and assume the beer must belong to him. The black man must be guilty! Is that how it is? Why does the beer have to belong to him?" I replied that he was the closest one to it. "What if it belongs to someone else?" "Okay, if the beer isn't his, then whose beer is it?" The same woman with the chip on her shoulder continued "It's all of ours! All three of us are drinking beer here in the park!" (excluding the dog owner who was not in the same proximity). "Well then, I need your I.D. and your

I.D." pointing to both females, and they both handed them to me. The same smart aleck piped up again and asked how they were supposed to know that alcohol was illegal in the parks. I told her that there was a sign at the entrance in English and Spanish. "Go show me!" she demanded. I said that she could go see it after she received her ticket. I asked the dog owner for his I.D., and he asked "Why?" as he retrieved it from his car. I informed him that every city had a leash law for public safety. Now they all began to ask why they couldn't have a warning instead of a ticket. I said that in Dallas we didn't have warning tickets, only verbal warnings. They still pestered me about a warning as I wrote their citations. I candidly told them that with their bad attitudes that I wouldn't give them a warning, just four tickets. Miss Bad Attitude asked me for my name, and I said that it would be on the ticket. She stood up and walked toward me and leaned forward as she read my name tag aloud. She mispronounced it, so I corrected her. She butchered my last name again several more times to get under my skin. She said that she wanted it for her complaint, because I had nothing better to do than harass black people. I asked her if she wanted to speak to a supervisor, but she declined and said that she'd take care of it herself. The three who had been at the table now told me that I should only write the male the ticket, because he admitted that the beer belonged to him. I told them that was exactly what I was going to do until I was corrected and told that they were all drinking beer from that bottle. I inquired about the address for the ticket I was writing for one of the men. When I heard the address number and street, I knew that there was an apartment number associated with it because there were only apartment buildings for several blocks there. The same loudmouth just had to make another racially charged remark with "Oh, so because we're black we have to live in an apartment and not a house!" I explained my rationale for the comment. They all took their time looking the tickets over before signing and handing them back to me. In my opinion, being a troublesome quartet, they deserved those tickets. I facetiously said, "Ya'll have a good day!" as I rode away, to which the usual spokeswoman replied "We hope you have a terrible day!" and they all laughed.

As a Courtesy Officer for an apartment complex, I had to sometimes take answering service calls in the middle of the night to earn my reduction in rent. I had only been in bed about 20 minutes when they phoned me and stated that a strange man was pounding on a woman's door wanting to get inside. I quickly dressed and was at her apartment within 10 minutes. Despite the short lapse of time, the unknown man was no longer banging on her door. He was lying in front of it, sound asleep, and snoring. I lightly patted him several times on his stomach with my flashlight to awaken him, but he was out like a light. I decided that he was probably drunk but was calm and peaceful being unconscious. I let him sleep in case he became belligerent and unruly when he regained consciousness. I awaited the arrival of two police officers that I had requested who would transport him to Detox. They showed within 5 minutes, and I informed them of the situation. I woke the man up by slapping him in the face rather hard about 10 times. One of the officers handcuffed him, and they were on the verge of going when we heard a female voice that came from another apartment, the one directly above us. The sot was her husband. We got her info and released him into her custody.

There are several dangerous jobs, and being a Law Enforcement officer is of course one of them. Each year, @ two hundred Peace Officers die in the line of duty in the USA, most by accidents and firearms. Dallas being a large city always had between @2500-3500 officers employed during my 26-year career 1990-2016. Obviously, a larger city population generally translates to higher rates of crime, and more danger for the officers. During my career, 25 Dallas officers died on duty. A large city can't just have all their police officers attend a funeral, so usually officers who did not know the officer who died answered 911 calls in the Patrol Division where the officer worked so that his co-worker friends could attend the funeral service. All officers from large cities to small towns have the safety of the public as their purpose, so we feel a natural brotherhood, a common bond with each other. This bond and the reality that survival to retirement is never guaranteed brings empathy, sympathy, and compassion from police agencies that are often hundreds of miles away. They assign an officer, or officers in multiple police cars to represent their city and police department to convey honor and respect for the fallen. It is relatively common for an officer involved in a line of duty death to have more than 100 police cars in his or her funeral procession. Especially impressive is when a deceased officer has a police car involved representing the hometown where he grew up, no matter how small. When all these cars are combined with the personal vehicles of family, friends, and relatives, the funeral procession can be miles long. At many points along the way from the church to the cemetery, mourners and well-wishers are stopped on the side of the road and people are atop bridges waving the American flag to display their respect and appreciation for the officer sacrifice. Sad to say, but the strongest silent majority support for Law Enforcement is most felt and evident after the tragedy of an officer death.

All the officer funerals in Dallas have a motorcycle escort to block off intersections enroute to the cemetery, an Honor Guard, a Police Choir, rifle/pistol volley salute, a bagpiper, and someone to play Taps on a bugle. Some of the funeral processions are so long, and the cemetery too small to accommodate the possibly hundreds of vehicles that there have been times when the cemetery service has ended when many cars in the procession have not yet even made it to the cemetery.

A suspect from a shooting call was last seen in a park/wooded area/bike trail area that was a part of my patrol division. I was miles away at White Rock Lake but decided that I could be of assistance by searching that area upon my arrival on my police bicycle. I arrived at the approximate area where the suspect was last seen and rode around and spied a lone man standing just off the bike trail and looking toward a field, watching me and a few police cars that had gather nearby. He knew something was happening but seemed to have no purpose just standing there. Our suspect had not yet been seen since his disappearance in the area, so I asked this male if he had seen our suspect and gave him a description. He hesitated to speak, and when he did, his comment unnerved me. He asked me "Why? What did he do?" He was of the same race as our suspect, and I was of the impression that in his mind it had to be a viable enough reason for us to get his cooperation. I told him that he had shot two people. Now he pointed to the field in front of some woods and told me "He ran in there." I alerted the dispatcher that the witness had told me that our armed suspect was hiding in a field and provided the location. Three officers came running from a different wooded area 100 yards away to assist me in the search. I was disgusted to see that several other officers who had parked on a street from the opposite direction just watched from outside their vehicles. They were content to do a very limited perimeter security to apparently prevent an escape in that direction rather than disperse. Some of them should've come over to help us find our armed suspect in the meadow. After the four of us scoured the meadow with pistols in our hand for a short time, I expanded our search to include the adjacent wooded area along a creek. After I walked alone a few minutes, one of the officers stumbled upon the suspect lying on the ground near a fallen log. I hustled over while he had the suspect at gunpoint, but by the time I arrived the suspect was already in custody. The young suspect had the Aggravated Assault weapon in one of his pockets. He was quick to tell us that he knew the law, and ludicrously informed us that the pistol didn't belong to him so we couldn't charge him with the shootings. Despite his self-serving knowledge of the law, he was subsequently charged with the shootings when he went to jail.

One of my rookies and I went to Narcotics for a briefing on a raid that was going to take place at a drug house within our patrol division. Afterward, we drove several miles down the highway. To make sure that all the officers who were to participate in the raid were still together, we met at a location nearer to the targeted house. Once all assembled, we resumed our travel hastily for the final few blocks and quickly halted at the front of the house. The front door was breached with a heavy metal "Doorknocker", and a couple of loud "flash-bangs" were lobbed inside the drug house to disorient everyone present there. My rookie and I had the duty of watching for any runners evacuating the house from the front or the east side. We heard many shouts from Narcotics officers inside yelling at suspects to get their hands up. Though it was dark outside, we could still see a heavy smoke drifting from the east windows. About that time, I spotted the silhouette of a moving head seeming to ride on the top of the smoke and wondered if it was friend or foe. It disappeared into the darkness heading east. Seconds later, a woman from the first house to the east ran out to the street in her bathrobe and stopped to look our way. She motioned for us to come there and while we ran toward her, she sounded off in a stifled scream that a man had just run into her garage. We told her to stay out on the street where there were several officers and told the dispatcher of the development. We entered the garage with pistols drawn and flashlight beams scanning all over the interior, but he wasn't seen, which meant he could only be in one place. He wasn't inside the woman's car, but our flashlights lit him up for us to see him under it. My rookie was on the side of the suspect's feet and did a great job of speedily yanking him out from under the vehicle just as I made it over to his side and the suspect was rapidly handcuffed. We obtained the neighbor's information and took our prisoner to the Narcotics division for interrogation and processing.

While I was waiting at a signal light, I noticed up ahead down the street that some vehicles were stopping and slowing and moving away from the middle lane. When the middle lane was fully vacated, I saw that the cars had moved to avoid hitting a small brown dog. He had already been struck once and was severely injured. My light changed to green, and I stopped behind the poor pooch to shield him and flipped on my emergency lights. I got out of my car and saw that a few other people had already came to the dog's aid, but the dog was in shock, pain and very frightened, and was snapping at their helping hands. The dog struggled to stand on his front legs, and then dragged his motionless hind section off to the right side of the road where he collapsed along the curb; his back or his hip was broken. All of us felt helpless. The sight of that suffering dog that had to be in excruciating pain was difficult to watch. I heard someone say, "the officer will help him", but I just envisioned myself pulling out my pistol and putting the poor pup out of his agonizing misery. A boy of about 11 or 12 showed up on the far side of this six-lane road and said aloud that it was his dog. Still upset over the dog's miserable condition, I scolded him that his dog was just hit by a car because he neglected to have him on a leash. The boy crossed over being followed by his two other unleashed dogs, but being daylight, drivers had slowed to watch as they passed by, and his other dogs were not struck because the motorists were attentive. The boy scooped up his maimed pet to bring him home for what I presumed was either a quick death at home or euthanasia from a Vet visit.

I worked an accident on North Central Expressway involving a motorist who had been driving a truck that had roughly a few dozen crates of strawberries on it (I don't remember the exact total). He was transported to the hospital for his injuries. I counted the crates of strawberries and did it again and arrived at the same number. It was a good thing that I double-checked the count. The driver who owned all those strawberries went to our Auto Pound a day or two later to reclaim his vehicle and the strawberries and reported that some crates were missing. He filed a written complaint with Internal Affairs over a theft, which went to our Public Integrity Unit. The allegation actually involved an Officer who worked at the Auto Pound who wrongly assumed that no one would want the strawberries because surely, they would rot before anyone returned for the vehicle and fruit crates. She was wrong. I was called and was at first simply asked if I was sure about the strawberry crate count, because the owner had claimed some were missing. I assured him of my accuracy as I had done it twice. Then they told me the reason. That Police Officer was terminated when the investigation was completed.

Shortly after starting our shift, we went across the street on our bicycles from the storage unit to the 7-Eleven. There we found out from a clerk that about an hour earlier that a man had ran out with a 30-pack of beer, ran behind an adjacent business, and hopped on the motorcycle of a waiting accomplice and fled. The clerk had tried to obtain the MC plate but could not. An outside customer had observed the theft and drove to catch up with the motorcycle. He wrote down the license plate and returned to give it to the appreciative clerk.

Normally, this incident at a convenience store would simply be reported on one of their Gas Drive off/Theft forms, but we knew the owner. He always conversed with us and took care of us. The registration returned to several blocks away and in a different Patrol Division, but a straight shot west from our location and then off into a neighborhood. We decided to confront the thieves. We found their residence to be 1 of 5 apartments within a house and saw that the front door was wide open. This allowed us to make legal entry via a welfare check. When there was no response, we made entry. The untidy apartment had a gas stove left on for heat, so we knew that the occupant would return soon. A neighbor asked us what was wrong and told us that the man just left on his motorcycle with his friend on the back, and that the friend lived at the back of the house in another unit. We decided to park nearby with our windows down so that we could hear them return. After 10 minutes, we wondered if maybe we somehow never heard the motorcycle and decided to take a gander. We pulled up and looked across three yards, and there was the MC owner out front. He didn't see us, so we turned the corner and stepped out, walking over to him. As we did, the other suspect walked from the back of the house and saw us approaching. He reversed course. I ran to him and told him to stop, because he was only getting a ticket. He in turn reiterated what I had said to an unseen person and declared "The officer said we're only getting a ticket". I ran to him and told him to put his hands up on a wall, and my partner who was just behind me started to pat him down. My attention was focused on the backyard, where I now saw a suspect in a black leather jacket next to the MC with reported license plates from the theft. This male still had a can of Keystone Light beer in his hand (the stolen beer brand), and tried to throw the beer can, but it comically hit the inside of the home's chain link fence and fell back into the yard. He ran over to the can and tried to dispose of the evidence again by tossing it, this time heaving it across the alley over a wooden fence into someone's backyard. He wasn't even close to doing this unnoticed by me. At first, he was uncooperative and adamant that he had loaned his MC to a friend, then admitted that he had done the theft but that he didn't want to reveal his name. The other officer overheard this and asked his suspect who had gone with him to steal the beer his name. He told the officer that he didn't want to tell him. The officer then took the scruff of his shirt into one of his fists and hoisted him upwards. With the suspect's back now against the fence, and his feet dangling off the ground, the officer told him that he was going to tell him the name of the other suspect. He let the man down, then walked with him to the front of the house out of sight of his friend and he gave the other officer the other name we needed. Both men received a citation for M/C Theft. My suspect received another citation for Littering on private property. He was a known sex offender, having had sex with a 14-year-old girl. He was 52. Though the crime occurred only a year earlier, he was somehow no longer in jail.

I was working a Violent Crime Task Force shift one night for overtime and was driving in the direction of my assigned territory to patrol. While at a red light, I noticed that the male directly in front of me had his seatbelt buckle dangling to his left. I thought I would give him a chance to fasten his seatbelt when he became aware of my presence. The light changed, and we drove for a couple of blocks. Still not fastening his seatbelt, I pulled him over. He said that he knew that he wasn't wearing his seatbelt, but that he didn't think that the government should tell him that he needed to wear it, that it should be a matter of personal choice. I informed him that whether he liked or disliked the law, it still existed, and that I did not enact the laws but that I did enforce them, and that he needed to put on his seatbelt. I returned to my vehicle expecting that my warning would be incentive enough for him to comply with the law. I soon realized after following him for a few more blocks down the same road that he had no intention of wearing that seatbelt. I stopped him again and wrote the stubborn fool a no seatbelt citation. All he had to do was wait until he or I turned off and then remove his seatbelt, but he had to make a (costly) point to prove his disdain for that law.

If people truly support Law Enforcement and want to lower crime in their community, they should be cooperative and helpful by supporting the police in this endeavor. The race of a criminal or suspect should be irrelevant and not determine whether you assist officers trying to perform their duties. If too many people are unwilling to take an active role as stakeholders in suppressing crime in their own community by being our eyes and ears, they shouldn't blame the police when their community has high crime levels. Citizens and the police need to function as a team with a shared goal of crime reduction.

I was in a foot pursuit with a suspect inside an apartment complex. As he ran outside of the complex, he turned to the right and had to have passed a bus stop shelter that was right there. I turned right and asked the people inside the shelter which way my suspect had ran, as I no longer had sight of him. Strangely, not one of those several people knew what I was talking about and had not seen anybody. They were all the same race as my suspect.

Weeks later, I was looking for a male suspect of a different race on a bicycle who I knew had to have passed that same bus shelter, once again occupied by people of the same one race. I pulled my squad car alongside the bus shelter to describe the man. This time they were all ever so cooperative and involved by pointing and verbally telling me his direction of travel, which resulted in his apprehension and arrest.

I stopped a man for speeding days before Thanksgiving and decided to give him a warning. A month later just before Christmas, I stopped him for speeding again in the exact same place. I thought that he looked familiar and reminded him that I was the one that gave him a warning for speeding one month earlier. "That was you?' came his reply. He received a ticket.

A young teenage girl had driven to a pharmacy to buy some items on my police beat. She didn't make it home, and her parents reported her missing. Her vehicle was found to still be in the pharmacy parking lot. Perplexed, officers reviewed the outdoor surveillance tape video. The girl had left the store and was approached by a man (suspect) who either threatened her or lied to her to coax her into his vehicle. It was daylight. She made no scream or attempt to run away and entered his car for an unknown reason. Did she do it willingly reacting to his having misled her with a lie? Did the suspect threaten harm to her or a loved one if she didn't comply with his demands? We didn't know. What we did know was that later her body was found on my beat. She was just inside a strip of woods along a creek found by a man who was walking his dog just blocks from her home. She had been raped and bludgeoned to death. It was a brutal, senseless tragedy that took the life of an innocent, nice girl and frightened the neighborhood. I don't know if this homicide case was solved.

I saw a male sitting on a folding chair on a boat ramp with his unleashed dogs roaming all over the place in this crowded park parking lot. I called to him and told him that his dogs needed to be on a leash. He replied "Okay", but then just sat there. I asked if he had some leashes, and he stated that they were in his truck, but then just sat there. I told him that his dogs needed to be on a leash, but he just called them over to him and put a hand on each dog's shoulder, as he just sat there. I stated what should be obvious and told him that he needed to get up and get his leashes from his truck. He shot me a look like I'M the jerk. His dogs ran off again even though he commanded them to return. I retrieved his ID and wrote him one ticket for violation of the city leash law. When he realized that he was getting a citation, he told me that I just "want to be a hard ass." I informed him that if I was trying to be a hard ass, then I would write him two tickets for his unleashed dogs instead of one and arrest him for his single ticket warrant out of the Dallas County Sherriff's office and have Animal Control take his two dogs. As he signed his ticket and received his copies, he still had to take a final verbal jab and declare that I was just being a hard ass.

A couple of hours later at 9:30p.m., I drove to the top of an area called Flagpole Hill. Here despite the darkness, I could see from my headlights that a very large group of mostly males had gathered under the park pavilion, with many cars parked all around it and on the grass as they listened to music in their cars and socialized with each other, many while drinking beer. Most were casually dressed, but a few wore the cultural attire of an unknown African nation, so it was a party with others from the same country of origin. As I neared, all that was visible to them at first were my headlights. Coming closer, I was no longer incognito, and several males identified my police car coming their way. One unlucky male was directly in the beams of my headlights, and it was comical to see him scrambling and twisting and turning to try to get rid of the beer bottle in his hand. He tried to put it on a car floorboard inside an open driver door, but the seated owner pushed him away. The beer holder just froze like a deer in the headlights, unable to dispose of the evidence for his knowingly violating the city ordinance banning alcohol in city parks. I stepped out and approached him as he spun around still trying to discard the beer in his hand. I told him that I would take that beer, and after he handed it to me, I poured it out. I obtained his ID and began to write him a ticket. A minute later, I noticed that he was walking away from me. I followed and told him to get back over here. He ignored me and kept walking. I followed him about 30 yards until he stopped to speak with a friend at another vehicle. I told him not to walk away from me, and his angry and illogical reply was that he didn't walk away from me. I pointed at where I first contacted him, and how now he was over here, that he did walk away. His response was that he didn't walk away, why would he walk away from me when I had his ID? I finished writing him the ticket and then asked him to sign at the X. He asked what it was for, and I told him it was an alcohol in the park violation. He stated that he wasn't going to sign it. I took the ticket book back from his hands and wrote "Refused to sign" on the signature line and gave him his ticket copies. As I turned to walk back to my cruiser, I heard him say "Faggot!" I couldn't actually do anything about this other than to turn and confront him, which I did, and queried "What did you call me?" He hesitated, then said that he had said "Bag it!", which made absolutely no sense. I turned to walk away and passed by a couple of males sitting in an open car. I heard them say something derogatory to me but couldn't make out what it was. I continued walking back to my police cruiser and now noticed that the ticket recipient was following me from a short distance. He was still dwelling on how I could say that he walked away when he didn't. I told him that he did, that he had his ticket copies, and that we were done here. I got back into my car, and he stopped from several yards away and declared "You're killing people!", to which I replied that I wasn't killing anyone. He reiterated "You be killing people!" From my open window, I told him what most people should know which is that people of any race are mostly killed by people of the same race when I replied "92% of blacks are killed by other blacks!" Then I began to drive away. I heard him shout back "Lies! Lies!"

The media has been known to perpetuate falsehoods or exaggerations about police bias or racial animus. They fail to distinguish one police agency from another (there are almost 18,000 police agencies in the United States—Wikipedia), and paint all of us with the same broad brush which is typically criticism and very seldom praise.

At times the media shows their own bias against the police by making false assumptions or conclusions, or an otherwise revealing insight. I remember once a News Helicopter was filming a Dallas Police car chase when a reporter aboard the chopper made what she thought was an off-microphone comment and said, "I hope he gets away." Another time, an off-duty Dallas Police officer was patrolling his apartment complex at night because he was a "Courtesy officer" there and received discounted rent. He came upon two suspects who were burglarizing a vehicle and pulled out his pistol to confront them. One of the suspects had a shotgun and blasted one time, striking the officer in the face and killing him. The officer was able to fire one bullet just moments before his fatal wound, and one of the suspects was struck and injured. The officer lived within the boundaries of the same Patrol Division where he worked, and his death occurred on what would've been his normal shift had he not been off. The first officers on the scene after they were called were officers that knew him well because they worked with him several days a week. A blood trail was eventually found and followed, and the wounded suspect was taken into custody. A news crew was present from a distance, and they filmed these officers when they lifted the suspect to put him on an ambulance stretcher. Officers are not unfeeling robots. The officer that this murderer killed was their friend. They hoisted him up and shoved him down onto the padded stretcher. I was watching TV news from home and was shocked to hear the insensitive and unsympathetic reporter make a cold-hearted callous comment at this action by saying "Watch now as the Dallas police launch a furious assault on the suspect!" I was upset and called the news station to file a complaint. They were in cover up and damage control mode. They may have only showed that news film comment once or twice, but enough people must have phoned to express their shock at the comment that they simply denied that it ever happened.

Impartial news is hard to come by nowadays. Rare is the journalist who presents all the facts without inserting his personal viewpoint on the matter rather than let readers decide on their own from being fully informed. Be aware that most all people have some kind of internal bias regarding subjects because few are 100% informed of all the involved facts. The news media may have an axe to grind and a narrative to perpetuate. They could simply report fake news or twist and distort facts by leaving out pertinent applicable facts from the other opposite side of a discussion not wanting to make their case for them. Expand your knowledge and do your own research to include relevant data and statistics to arrive at the whole truth so that you can make an educated and informed decision on any given subject. Far too many hastily jump to conclusions when they know so little truth about an event.

INTERESTING FACTS AND CRIME DATA SOURCES

Fewer than half of crimes in the U.S. are reported and fewer than half of reported crimes are solved—Pew Research Center

Auto thefts are the most likely crime to be reported. Murders are the most likely crime to be solved, or "cleared" by an arrest, 61% of the total. —Pew research Center

In descending order, the greatest numbers of arrests in the U.S. are for drug violations, DWI/DUI, and Larceny/Theft. —FBI Persons Arrested Criminal Justice Information Services Division

Vermont has had the fewest police officer deaths in the line of duty with 29. Texas has had the most with 2,288 line of duty deaths since statehood in 1845 (includes 176 from Covid19). — ODMP

In 2021, there were 660,000 FULL TIME Law Enforcement Officers in the USA (includes local, county, state, and federal). —Statista

There is an average police agency turnover rate of 14%, with some departments struggling with an annual turnover rate of 20%--National Police Foundation, August 1, 2023

Intimidation (name calling and graffiti) was the most reported Hate Crime in 2021, 43% of the total. Add in hate crimes from simple assaults (push, slap, punch, etc.) and the two categories represent 78% of the total. White Americans are the most common perpetrators of hate crimes being 59% of the U.S. population and 52% of the total hate crimes. Black Americans are 13% of the U.S. population and 22% of the hate crime perpetrators. —usafacts.org

In 2020 there were 10,528 victims of hate crimes in the USA (FBI 2020 Hate Crime Statistics), out of a total of 7.75 MILLION reported crimes (1.3 million violent crimes and 6.45 million property crimes)—Statista. That is a statistically insignificant 1 hate crime for every 736 crimes that are reported.

Between 1982 and August 2023, 78 of 147 mass shootings (FBI defines that as a shooting with at least 4 victims) were committed by Whites, and 26 mass shootings were by African Americans. —Statista Research Dept. Sept 5,2023. Whites with 59% of the population committed 53% of mass shootings, while African Americans with 13% of the national population were responsible for 18% of the total mass shootings. In over half of mass shootings since 1982, the shooter showed previous signs of mental illness. —Statista

These Government publications are most useful for finding the truth about crimes, arrest statistics and wanted persons:

Bureau of Justice Statistics.gov

FBI.gov

FBI's Crime Data Explorer (to find crime stats for your state, county, or town)

The FBI also has lists for the 10 Most Wanted Fugitives, Terrorists, Kidnappings & Missing Persons, ECAP (shows the faces of unknown adults active in the sexual abuse of children and child pornography), and VICAP (Violent Criminal apprehension Program)

Incarceration in the United States (includes demographics)- Wikipedia

Milton Keynes UK
Ingram Content Group UK Ltd.
UKHW011910060524
442290UK00001B/106

9 798218 378